Egypt's Destiny

A PERSONAL STATEMENT BY

Mohammed Naguib

DOUBLEDAY & COMPANY, INC.

GARDEN CITY, NEW YORK, 1955

Library of Congress Catalog Card Number 55-5271

Printed in the United States
At the Country Life Press, Garden City, N.Y.
Designed by Alma Reese Cardi
First Edition

EDITOR'S NOTE

It is impossible to be consistent in transliterating Arabic into English without resorting to the use of a phonetic system that would be too elaborate for the purposes of this book. According to the simple but imperfect system used herein, vowels are pronounced as in Spanish or Italian (except in such familiar words as *shaikh*). Consonants are pronounced as in English. The acute accent (′) indicates the syllable to be stressed in words that foreigners often mispronounce. The apostrophe indicates the important but, to foreigners, almost unpronounceable glottal consonant, *'ein,* or *'ain.* Colloquial words have been used in preference to literary words, and an effort has been made in the spelling of all words to approximate the pronunciation of Lower Egypt.

ACKNOWLEDGMENT

THE AUTHOR ACKNOWLEDGES WITH THANKS THE
EDITORIAL ASSISTANCE OF LEIGH WHITE.

CONTENTS

EGYPT'S DESTINY
A PERSONAL STATEMENT

1

THE LOST WAR

When the calf is thrown, as we say in Arabic, the knives begin to fall. So many knives have fallen on King Faruk already that I can take no pleasure in adding to their number here. I would prefer to ignore the past and confine myself to the present and the future. But since the present begins in the past, as the future begins in the present, I must begin my story by casting a backward glance at the sorry reign of the deposed King of Egypt.

In 1936, when young Faruk Fuad ascended the throne left vacant on the death of his father, Ahmed Fuad, I prayed to God that he might prove to be the exemplary ruler that our suffering country so badly needed. Faruk, in Arabic, means One Who Carefully Distinguishes between Right and Wrong. As the years went by, however, it became increasingly apparent that Faruk was incapable of living up to his name. Far from being a better ruler than his father, he was so much worse that in time Fuad's name began to acquire an unmerited luster. The nadir of Faruk's

reign was reached in 1948. In that year, while Egypt was embroiled in a hopeless war in Palestine, he chose to divorce his
Queen in a double ceremony in which the young Shah of Iran,
Mohammed Rizah, also divorced his Empress, who was one of
Faruk's five sisters. Faruk, though he was only twenty-eight at the
time, had degenerated to such an extent that he no longer knew
or cared where his interests lay. Corruption ruled in every public
office. Egypt had become the epitome of all that was wrong with
the Eastern world.

Egyptian landowners, instead of paying their taxes, bribed the
civil service to accept a fraction of what they owed the government. Instead of investing their savings, legal or illegal, in productive enterprises in Egypt, they either exported their savings or
invested them in inflated urban and rural real estate. The result
was a land boom in the midst of unprecedented suffering on the
part of the great majority of Egypt's 22,000,000 people—suffering that an irresponsible, corrupt, and impoverished government
was neither willing nor able to remedy.

The laws of economics were as perverted as the laws of men.
Rising prices in the towns and cities were accompanied by rising
unemployment. Except in the building trades, there were few jobs
open to anyone, and there were almost no jobs open in any field
to the increasing numbers of young people graduating from the
high schools and universities. Conditions in the countryside were
even worse. The higher the price of cotton, the higher the price of
land; and the higher the price of land, the higher the rents exacted
from the tenant farmers, whose real income was shrinking with
every month that passed.

Justice hid its head. Men who were honest and courageous
enough to attempt to improve conditions were continually being
thwarted. A few were to be found in every profession, but, for

reasons peculiar to Egypt, they were most numerous among the military. Except for the royal family, there was no aristocracy, and the landowners' and traders' sons who might have led the Armed Forces were too busy enjoying their wealth to be bothered with military service. The officers' corps in consequence was largely composed of the sons of civil servants and soldiers and the grandsons of peasants. I was myself the grandson of a peasant on one side of my family and the grandson of a colonel on the other. My father was an Egyptian Army captain employed in the Sudan civil service. We officers, though no longer peasants ourselves, were deeply in sympathy with the plight of the peasants whose sons made up our ranks. A few of us, of course, had been corrupted by bribery and lost to the national cause. But the great majority remained true to our calling, which was the defense of the nation, and for that reason we were more incensed than other professional groups at what was happening to our country.

The purpose of the military is not to govern but to defend those who govern from their enemies, foreign and domestic. There have been times in the history of almost every country, however, when it has become impossible for the military to remain aloof from politics. To serve its purpose, the military must be given a worthy government to defend. If the government it is asked to defend is manifestly indefensible, as it was in Egypt, the military must either resign itself to the prevailing corruption or intervene in civil affairs long enough to establish a government that will respond to the legitimate needs and desires of the nation.

This is what the military movement has attempted to do in Egypt. We seized power because we could no longer endure the humiliations to which we, along with the rest of the Egyptian people, were being subjected. For most of us the breaking point was our inexcusable defeat in Palestine, but for some of us it occurred much earlier. My own breaking point was reached in 1942, when King Faruk surrendered to a dictatorial British ambassador, Sir Miles Lampson (now Lord Killearn), who had surrounded his palace with troops and tanks. I was then a lieutenant colonel of infantry. The King refused to accept my proffered resignation, and from then on I remained in the Army more or less against my will.

Lampson's shabby treatment of the King of Egypt was but one of many factors that eventually caused us to revolt. Ibrahim Attallah's abuse of his authority was another. General Attallah, our Chief of Staff, was a nepotist and playboy who shamelessly accepted gifts from those who wanted favors done at the Army's expense. He rewarded those of his subordinates who were willing to flatter his vanity and humiliated those whose self-respect prevented them from doing so. The result was the abortive conspiracy organized by Mohammed Rashad Mehanna in 1947.

Mehanna, who was then a major of artillery, was thirty-nine years old. I was a full colonel at the time and all of forty-six. I was therefore thought to be much too old to be taken into the plotters' confidence. Had they seen fit to consult me, however, I would have opposed their plot on the ground that it was premature. They lacked the popular following necessary to succeed. I was engaged, moreover, in a conspiracy of my own—a conspiracy to unite the Egyptians and the Sudanese in an effort to free both countries from British tutelage—and I feared that Mehanna's conspiracy would only delay the results that my friends and I, in our own way, were working to achieve.

Mehanna's plot was eventually discovered by Attallah's spies. The conspirators were arrested, but the charges against them were never pressed, presumably for fear of revealing the corruption that flourished in the Army's supply services. Mehanna and his henchmen were released and Attallah was retired in the hope of restoring the Army's morale in time for Egypt to intervene successfully in Palestine. Unfortunately, Attallah's successor as Chief of Staff, Osman el Mahdi, was so afraid of incurring the King's displeasure that he failed even to investigate, much less prosecute, the grafters who would contribute so heavily to our defeat.

II

I was opposed to a formal war in Palestine and said so at every opportunity. There was nothing to be gained and much to be lost by demonstrating our military weakness. We would have done better, in my opinion, to confine ourselves to guerrilla operations in support of the internal Arab resistance movement. Jewish immigration would have been discouraged, and there would have been no excuse, in the absence of formal intervention, for either recognizing Israel or imposing an embargo on the sale of arms to the various Arab states. We might not have won the war, but at least we would not have lost it as decisively as we did. All we achieved by intervening openly in Palestine was to make it possible for the Zionists to assume the fictional but effective role of a persecuted minority fighting for its life.

The war itself was largely a series of truces interspersed with minor battles. Time and again I was forced to hold my fire while the Jews delivered munitions to the front in the guise of supplies for isolated settlements of colonists. I particularly remember a shipment of "cosmetics" that turned out to be mines and hand grenades. Once, during a truce, I insisted on inspecting a convoy of forty-two trucks that was supposed to be carrying legitimate supplies to a settlement in southern Negeb. Each truck carried half a dozen "spare" tires and as many drums of "spare" gasoline. Two officers representing the United Nations, an American and a Frenchman, were present. It was easy enough to tell from the size, shape, and weight of some of the boxes in the trucks that they contained munitions. But the UN officers refused to halt the convoy, and I was forbidden to seize its contents while the truce was in effect. I reported back to my superiors, who formally protested to the United Nations, but to no avail. Hardly a day passed without a truce violation of the sort that I have described. The enemy was also allowed to receive munitions by air.

Between truces we fought as well as we could with the limited amounts of poor equipment at our disposal. Many of our British guns and mortars could not be used for lack of shells. Many of our American tanks were crippled for lack of spare parts. The hand grenades that we received from Italy were so poorly made that many of them blew up in our soldiers' faces. A belated shipment of Spanish field guns turned out to be rejects that could not have been used effectively even if they had arrived in time. The rifles that we received from Spain were Mausers dating from 1912. They were all right for training purposes, but they were of little use against the automatic Czech, Russian, and American weapons with which the enemy was supplied.

In September 1949 a series of mysterious explosions destroyed our ammunition dumps in the Mokattam Hills outside of Cairo. The explosions confirmed what we had suspected all along— namely, that several of our supply officers, in league with the King and his cronies, had been buying substandard munitions and pocketing the difference between what they had charged the government and what they had actually paid.

Is it any wonder that the Egyptian Army made such a poor showing in Palestine?

It is not my purpose to make excuses for anyone but the Egyptian soldier. I am sure that, given the proper training and leadership, he will fight as well as any soldier in the world, as indeed he did, a century ago, when the Egyptian Army under Ibrahim Pasha succeeded in conquering half the Ottoman Empire. Our defeat in Palestine was due, first, to international political factors that we could not control, and, second, to a corrupt internal regime that we had tolerated far too long. It was not due to any lack of courage on the part of the Egyptian soldier.

Early in 1948, before we had officially entered the war, I was a colonel in command of the 2nd Machine Gun Battalion at El Arísh, on the Mediterranean coast of Sinai. One day I was ordered to assemble a platoon of volunteers for service with the Arab guerrilleros in Palestine. I paraded my battalion and ordered all who wished to volunteer to step four paces forward. Every man but one responded. Some even threw themselves at my feet in gratitude for the opportunity I offered them to serve the Arab cause. The one man who failed to step forward was an Albanian, a professional gambler who had been making a good thing of his army life.

"Why are you standing there all alone?" I asked.

"I'm not a fool, sir. Why should I fight until I have to?"

"I can think of one reason," I said. "To show that Albanians are still brave men."

"Oh, in that case, sir, I'd better volunteer."

We all laughed as he, too, stepped four paces forward. The joke was that King Faruk was by way of being an Albanian too. His great-great-grandfather, Mohammed Ali, the founder of modern Egypt, was an Albanian who started out as a tobacco merchant in Greece and ended up as an autonomous Turkish viceroy with all the powers of a king.

I dismissed my men and informed Cairo that, instead of the thirty-one volunteers requested, my whole battalion of thirty-five officers and 817 men had volunteered.

It was not long afterward that I was promoted to the rank of brigadier and warned that the Egyptian Army would soon be entering Palestine in force. My task would be to act as second in command of the invading forces under Major General Ahmed Ali el Mawawi, a short, fat man who spoke with a lisp. I called his attention to the fact that only four of our battalions could be considered fit for battle. Mawawi shrugged.

"We have our orders," he said. "Our duty is to carry them out, not to question them."

"On the contrary, sir," I said. "Our duty is to question every order that can't be carried out. We're preparing to invade Palestine in force. You and I both know that it can't be done successfully with the men and materials at our disposal. Why court disaster?"

Mawawi reminded me that it was he and not I who was the GOC. I saluted and stalked out of his office. There was nothing more that I could do except to see that our soldiers fought as well as possible in the circumstances.

III

The Egyptian Army had been trained and commanded by Britons for two generations. Until 1936, when the Anglo-Egyptian Treaty of Friendship and Alliance was signed, the Army's British mentors had opposed every effort to make it an effective fighting force for fear that it might someday be used against them. Since 1936, to be sure, they had improved the quality of its training and equipment, but not to such an extent that it could be used effectively against the Zionists in Palestine.

It had long been my hope to imbue the Army with a new spirit, and I now proceeded to do so with a double purpose—first, to confound the King and his cronies, and, second, to confound the British. I was ashamed of the low esteem in which Egyptians were held by Britons and other foreigners, and I was determined to show our cynical rulers that something could and would be done about it. I therefore became a "soldiers' general." I made it absolutely clear to my men that I would ask them to do nothing that I was not prepared to do myself. I shared their food and slept in the open with them to show what I expected in the way of soldierly behavior. I punished the liars and the slovens and rewarded those who told the truth and kept their minds and bodies clean. I think I can say without boasting that the troops under my command fought better than any of the others. My men trusted me and I trusted them, which was as it should have been but seldom was, in an Army trained to serve British rather than Egyptian interests.

We entered the war with so little preparation that there was no time to carry out a general mobilization. I had to hire twenty-one trucks from Palestinian Arabs in order to haul my troops from Rafa up to Gaza, and I had to leave some of my six-pounders behind for lack of tractors. The terrain was too difficult to haul them behind our trucks. The officer in charge of the abandoned six-pounders cried for shame, and there were tears in my own eyes as well.

Between May and December I took part in twenty-one engagements. On each occasion I led my men into battle even though it was no part of my responsibility as a senior officer to do so. I wanted my subordinates to follow my example. Demoralization spreads from the top, not the bottom, of any organization. Hopeless though our predicament was, I was determined that it would be through no fault of mine that we should be defeated.

One reason why the Turks were victorious in Gallipoli, and why they were later able, after their crushing defeat, to repel the Greek invasion, was that Mustafa Kemál Atatürk and his fellow officers did the same. Kemál, who was never wounded in spite of all the risks he took, acquired the reputation of being invulnerable to bullets. In the beginning I, too, enjoyed the same sort of reputation. So many officers were killed at my side that I came to be known as "Bulletproof" Naguib. Many of my Sudanese troops believed that I carried an amulet around my neck; it was supposed to contain special verses from the Koran that protected me from death. But the law of averages soon took effect. Counting a grazed finger, I was wounded four times in seven months—the last time so seriously that I almost died. But, though I was no longer known as "Bulletproof," the mere fact that I survived was attributed by many of my men to the *baraka* that I was supposed to possess—a special blessing that had spared me for the accomplishment of some divine purpose. Although I don't really believe in my *baraka,* I have found it expedient to behave as if I did, as I think everyone in my position, to be successful, must. And who can say that the Revolution I was chosen to lead was not really a "blessed movement," as the people called it? Who knows but what God in His wisdom decided that the time had come for the children of the Nile, the Egyptians and the Sudanese, to take their destiny into their own hands at last?

In June, at Isdúd, just south of Tel Aviv, my forces won the largest battle in which Egyptians were engaged in Palestine. After three days of fighting we counted 450 enemy dead—more than a tenth of the 4000 Zionists who had opposed us. My own forces numbered 2300 and our casualties were relatively light.

A week later, after the Battle of Nitsanim, Mawawi cited me for bravery and recommended that I be either exceptionally promoted to the rank of major general or awarded the King Fuad Star, which was Egypt's highest military decoration. A mine had exploded two paces in front of me, and I had received a number of superficial wounds in my chest and right loin. I kept my wounds a secret from Mawawi for fear that he would use them as an excuse for sending me back to Cairo. I handed over the 2nd Infantry Brigade to its original commander, Brigadier Mahmúd Fahmi Nematallah, who had just arrived from Cairo, and returned to Gaza to undergo secret treatment. Two weeks later I was strong enough to resume my duties. In the meantime I had relieved Major General Mohammed Fawzi, who had fallen ill, as the commander of the 4th Infantry Brigade. Eventually I was placed in command of the sector running from Bethlehem to Faluga to Magdal on the Mediterranean.

In July, just before the second truce, my forces were badly defeated in the Battle of Negba. Mawawi had rejected my own plan of action in favor of one of his own, which was so faulty, in my opinion, that I refused to carry it out. He relieved me of my command, but, as soon as he realized that we were going to be defeated, he asked me to command our withdrawal, which I carried out in the midst of a series of unopposed enemy air attacks.

A few days later I appealed to Mawawi for reinforcements to make up for the heavy casualties that we had suffered. He refused to believe that our losses had been as great as I said they were and accused me of trying to blame him unjustly for our defeat. In front of several staff officers he berated me in terms that I could not accept, and so I demanded that he apologize. When he refused to do so I told him what I thought of him in terms as strong as those he had used in describing me. I then returned to my headquarters and drew up a written report of what had happened. I submitted it to Mawawi with the request that he apologize in writing. Instead he ordered me to report to GHQ in Cairo and recommended that I be tried for insubordination. His recommendation was never acted upon, however, because of its inconsistency with his previous recommendation that I be either exceptionally promoted or decorated with the Fuad Star.

IV

Back in Cairo I cursed myself for what I had allowed to happen. It was not the first time, nor the last, that I have had cause to regret my violent temper. All I achieved on this occasion was to place the entire responsibility for the war in Palestine on the inadequate shoulders of Mawawi. As for myself, I was placed in command of the Senior Officers' School. My superiors seemed to regard my new command as a sort of consolation prize, but I regarded it as a form of punishment, for I had expected to be either court-martialed or sent back to the front.

It was not until November, after a series of disastrous retreats, that Mawawi was at last relieved. Major General Ahmed Fuad Sadek was appointed to succeed him as the GOC in Palestine. Sadek in turn appointed me to command the 10th Infantry Brigade Group, which he intended to use as his main striking force, but it was only after he had threatened to resign that my appointment was approved.

A secret committee had previously been appointed to investigate my quarrel with Mawawi and what had happened since. The president of the committee was Faruk's brother-in-law, Ismail Sherín, the second husband of Princess Fawzía, the former

Empress of Iran. Sherín was an honorary colonel who owed his rank to his wife's position. He was a capable young man, even so, and I was grateful for his support. His committee submitted a report to the King in which it was recommended that I be decorated and promoted and that either I or Sadek or Major General Abbas Abd el Hamíd be named to succeed Mawawi as our GOC in Palestine. But, though the King reacted favorably, the Commander in Chief of the Armed Forces, Lieutenant General Mohammed Haidar, did not. He appointed Sadek to succeed Mawawi and vetoed both my promotion and my decoration on the ground that, after quarreling with Mawawi, I was not entitled to either.

My wife was in the hospital at the time, undergoing treatment for rheumatism, and so I stayed at home with our three sons while I awaited the promotion that Haidar had countermanded. In the meantime, however, Sadek had become so worried that he ordered me to return to the front immediately, regardless of my status. As I packed my kit and prepared to leave, I listened to an official radio broadcast in which it was announced that the King had just conferred on me the Fuad Star, in spite of Haidar's disapproval.

Although I was still only a brigadier, Sadek placed me in command of the 10th Infantry Brigade Group, which consisted of four infantry battalions plus artillery, tanks, engineers, and other auxiliary services. This was on November 19. Two weeks later he added the 4th Infantry Brigade to my command, thus making me the first Egyptian officer ever to command what amounted to a division in the field.

Isdúd and Magdal had long since been lost. Our front south of Bethlehem had been pushed back to a line running from Beersheba to Gaza on the Mediterranean.

On the night of December 22, 1948, the enemy broke through our lines south of Gaza between Deir el Balah and Khan Yunis, capturing Hill 86, from which height they were able to shell both villages. At dawn on December 23, using three companies and five tanks, I attempted to encircle Hill 86. All of the tanks stalled before they could overrun the enemy's positions. The automobile batteries with which they were equipped were not strong enough to start their engines more than a few times on a single charge. Each tank carried replacements, of course, but the time lost in exchanging batteries robbed us of the advantage of surprise.

One of the stalled tanks was caught in a cross fire from two enemy machine-gun emplacements. Only one member of the crew of three succeeded in emerging safely. The second was killed outright and the third, who had been wounded, was trapped inside, as I could tell from the way he struggled to escape.

Feeling responsible for his predicament, I left my jeep and driver and the staff officer who was accompanying us and crawled five hundred yards under heavy fire in the hope of pulling the wounded man out to safety. As I was lifting him out of the hatch, he was hit in the head and instantly killed by two machine-gun bullets, two more of which hit me before I could take cover behind the tank.

I lay on my back and unbuttoned my overcoat and blouse. Blood was bubbling out of a hole in my chest, and there was a burning pain in my right side. The hands of my watch indicated that it was now 7 A.M. It was broad daylight, and had been for several hours, but it seemed so dark that I was surprised to find that I could still tell the time.

At seven forty-five, after the other tanks had forced the enemy to withdraw, it was possible for Captain Gamál Sahber and two soldiers from the 7th Infantry Battalion to help me return to my jeep, whose driver had approached to within a hundred yards of where I had been lying. Sahber's men wanted to carry me, but I insisted on walking with my arms around their shoulders in order to conceal from the rest of my troops how badly wounded I really was. It is never good for the morale of soldiers to see their commander being carried off the battlefield.

At the company command post I explained what had happened and gave the necessary orders for continuing the battle. Brigadier Mahmúd Ra'afat, the commander of the sector, who was to take my place, asked me to forgive him for the bitter remark he had made as I was about to attack.

"May God send you a bullet," he had said, "if you get us into any more trouble than we're in already."

Although my wounds were causing an increasing amount of pain, I did my best to smile as I agreed to forgive him on one condition—namely, that he write down my testament and see that it reached my sons.

He wrote at my dictation, "Remember that your father died honorably and that his last desire was that you should avenge our defeat in Palestine and work for the unity and independence of the Nile Valley."

I must here ask Western readers to forgive me if my words seem quaint. We Moslems live with God, the same God as yours, and when we die it is our custom to leave our children an inspiring thought to remember as part of their family heritage. My wife still retains the message I sent to our children, although it was God's will that I should be spared to lead the Egyptian Revolution.

Enemy airplanes were bombing and strafing the regimental aid post at Deir el Balah when we arrived. I was accordingly driven back to our field hospital near Rafa on the old Egyptian border.

There, at nine o'clock, because I had no pulse, I was pronounced dead by the first surgeon who examined me.

Fortunately my body was soon discovered by Captain Saláh ed Din Sheríf, the commander of our medical transportation service. Captain Sheríf was a half brother of my friend and late comrade in arms, Colonel Ahmed Abd el Azíz, who had distinguished himself in the fighting at Bethlehem and Beersheba. On lifting the blanket that covered my face, and noticing that I blinked my eyes, Captain Sheríf called another surgeon, who succeeded in bringing me back to life with the help of adrenalin, a blood transfusion, and an oxygen tent. Later that day I asked General Sadek, who had come to see me, if we had won any sort of victory. With tears in his eyes he told me that we had. The Jews had been forced to abandon Hill 86. Khan Yunis and Deir el Balah for the time being were secure.

"Now," I said, "I can die happily."

But instead of dying I recovered. By April 1949 I was strong enough to leave the Aguza Military Hospital in Giza to join my family in the little house my wife had rented in the Cairo suburb of Helmíet el Zeitún. My survival was a miracle. One of the two bullets had cracked two of my right ribs. The other had perforated my left lung, grazed my heart, and emerged through my third left rib. The initial hemorrhage was soon stanched but the subsequent pleurisy lasted for several months. In the end, though, thanks to God, the Beneficent, the Merciful, I regained my normal health.

v

In June I was again placed in command of the Senior Officers' School. Although I had by then been twice decorated with the

Fuad Star, my promotion to the rank of major general was still being withheld. But I was in no mood to complain. I had survived wounds that might well have been fatal and I was becoming interested in a new secret organization that promised to bring about an Egyptian renaissance.

One of my former staff officers, a young major named Mohammed Abd el Hakím Amer, had often visited me in the hospital. Now he began to come to see me in my office at the Senior Officers' School. He told me that he and several of his friends were eager to erase the stigma of our defeat in Palestine and wanted me to advise them. I promised to help in every way I could. The officers with whom I had been associated since 1942 were now meeting regularly to discuss ways and means of forcing Faruk to purge the Army of the grafters who were still in control of our supply services. But we had yet to agree on a plan of action and I was beginning to lose my patience.

One day Amer brought a friend of his to see me. He was another young major whom I remembered having met at Faluga, in Palestine. His name was Gamál ed Din Abd el Nasser. I soon realized, though neither of them told me so, that Abd el Nasser was the leader of their organization and that he had come to see me in order to weigh Amer's estimation of my character. Abd el Nasser was then thirty-one; Amer was two years younger.

It was a strange reversal of roles for a senior officer to be examined, however respectfully, by two of his juniors, but I was not displeased. I was coming to the conclusion that Egypt's salvation depended on its junior officers. Even the best of our senior officers, with few exceptions, were lacking in determination. What was needed, I thought, was the fire of youth, checked by an older head.

Abd el Nasser seemed to agree with me. Before long he and

Amer began to call at my house by night. Sometimes I would be late for our appointments and would arrive to find Abd el Nasser's little car, a black Austin, waiting at the corner. My house is on Sharia Saíd, the last side street leading off Sharia Tumán Bai, which ends in a traffic circle a block away. On the traffic circle is a night club called the Helmía Palace. Whenever I was late, in order to avoid arousing the suspicions of the police, Abd el Nasser and Amer would pretend to be waiting for someone in the night club. Usually they came to see me alone, but sometimes they were accompanied by Saláh ed Din Salem, another young major, whose premature baldness made him look much older than his thirty years. Abd el Nasser, a dark man with a long, straight nose, was the largest and heaviest of the three. Amer, though tall, was thin and wiry, while Salem was about my size and weight. The three of them wore mustaches, as I did myself, and Salem, whose eyes were bothering him, often wore dark glasses.

After numerous meetings had revealed that we were in agreement on all basic issues, Abd el Nasser invited me to join the *Zubat el Ahrar,* or Free Officers, the secret organization of which he was the founder and president. I agreed to do so. Of the nine members of the original executive committee, I was to meet only five before the Revolution, and I was not to succeed Abd el Nasser as its president until after the burning of Cairo in January 1952. Abd el Nasser, as I later learned, had been hoping that General Sadek would also join the committee, in which event he would have become its president. But Sadek declined, for fear of compromising his position, and so, at Amer's insistence, I became the president of the Free Officers in his stead. If I had been as much of a public figure as Sadek was, following the Palestinian War, I would probably have declined myself. It would have done him no good in his open struggle with Haidar and the others to have been accused of plotting against the government. As it was, he was always sympathetic to our movement, and from time to time he gave us valuable assistance.

In August 1949, while still a brigadier, I was appointed director general of the Frontier Corps, the military side of which consisted of 3000 soldiers, mostly Sudanese, and ninety-six officers, mostly Egyptians. The civil side consisted of several hundred police officers and men plus the civilian administrators of the various deserts that make up ninety-seven per cent of the area of Egypt. The military side of the Frontier Corps, as I knew from experience, was the best of all our Armed Forces, and I was proud to return to it as its director general. I would have been happier, of course, if I had been promoted, but perhaps it was just as well that I failed to become a major general until 1950. Had I been promoted when I should have been, I might have become the Chief of Staff, and, as such, I would have had to defend the King against my will. As it was, I was so disgusted with his behavior by the time I became a full general that I was ready to revolt at any time. Hence my feeling that the King and his cronies, by delaying my promotion, were unconsciously preparing me for the role that I would be called upon to play in 1952. I was by then completely devoid of any sense of loyalty to a regime that had so often betrayed the Egyptian people.

Secret work was by no means new to me. I had been a member of one or another secret organization ever since 1919, and in 1923 I had joined the White Banner. This was a group that had helped to prevent the British from converting Egypt and Sudan into two separate colonies.

In joining the White Banner, I had sworn on the Koran to guard its secrets with my life. Secrecy among the Free Officers, however, was maintained solely on the basis of our military honor, and I am proud to say that, prior to the Revolution, not a single member proved unworthy of his trust. The Free Officers was in no sense a religious organization. Although the great majority of our members were practicing Moslems, as indeed were the great majority of the Egyptian people, we acted not as Moslems but as officers sworn to defend the honor and dignity of Egypt, a country in which the rights of national and religious minorities have long been respected.

So much for the charge that certain members of the executive committee were secret members of the *Ikhwan el Muslimún,* or Moslem Brotherhood. All of us, myself included, had friends among the *Ikhwan,* but except for Mehanna, who was never a member of the executive committee, we were opposed to the *Ikhwan's* objective of converting Egypt into a theocratic state.

The charges that we were acting under Fascist or Communist inspiration were equally unfounded. Those among us who were tainted with Communism were eventually removed. The one member of the committee who had worked with the Germans during the Second World War had done so because he was an enemy of the British occupiers of Egypt, not because he was an admirer of Adolf Hitler.

As for the charge that I was but a figurehead, the facts are as I have stated them. I joined the Free Officers in the summer of 1949 and became their president in the spring of 1952. Abd el Nasser, who had meanwhile been promoted to the rank of lieutenant colonel, realized that a successful revolution could not be carried out by a group of junior officers unless they were led by a senior officer with special qualifications. I was that senior officer. I was known to every man in the Army and could count on its support; my reputation was above reproach; and my personality was such as to appeal to the Egyptian people. As president of the executive committee, I acted as the movement's commander in chief; Abd el Nasser, who assumed the title of secretary general, acted as its chief of staff. Both of us were responsible to the committee, which later became the Council of the Revolution, and neither of us acted, for a long time, without its unanimous approval. Whenever differences arose between any of its members, they were referred to the Council as a whole. The Council would meet for as long as necessary to reach a unanimous decision, even though it sometimes took us ten or twelve hours to do so. The Council's decisions were final and, except toward the end, were never discussed outside its secret meetings. We were thus able, for nineteen months, to rise above the issue of personalities, so long the curse of Egyptian politics, and to work together as a disciplined unit in the interests of the nation as a whole.

35788

2

A SON OF THE NILE

In 1954, when this book was written, I was either fifty-three or fifty-five years old, depending on whether I was born, as I once thought, on June 28, 1899, or, as I now think, on February 20, 1901. The discrepancy arises from the fact that births, deaths, and marriages were not officially recorded in Sudan until just before the First World War. If anyone knew my exact age, it was my father, Yussef Naguib, but he died before I understood the position in our family of my brother Abbas. My mother, in trying to forget that Abbas existed, succeeded only in forgetting the year in which she became my father's wife. All she could remember was that I was born in Khartum about one year later.

My father kept a little notebook in which he recorded such events as the six battles in which he fought, the day he was wounded, and the day he killed a viper. On one page of the notebook was a list of dates that seemed to correspond with the births of nine of his ten children. But whether the list began with the birth of Abbas and ended before the birth of Mahmúd, my youngest brother, or whether it began with my own birth and ignored the birth of Abbas is a question that I have never been able to answer satisfactorily. All I know is that I was allowed to assume, until my father died, that I was born on June 28, 1899, the first date on the list. But after my father's death, when I finally realized that Abbas was my half brother and not my full brother, as I had thought, I began to wonder. Abbas himself was not very helpful. He was a simple *felláh,* or peasant, who had grown up in Naharía, my father's native village in Lower Egypt. Like most *fellahín,* he was unsure of the exact date of his birth. It seemed probable, though, from what little he could remember, that he was born in the Moslem lunar year that corresponded with the Christian solar year of 1899. If so, I was born myself in 1901.

My father fought under Kitchener and Wingate in the reconquest of Sudan. In 1898, following the occupation of Dongola, he married Saída Mohammed Hamza, a native of the ancient town of Meroë, or Maraweh as it is called today, about halfway between Khartum and Wadi Halfa. My father divorced her one year later. Unable to care for Abbas himself, he left the boy with his uncle, Kotb el Kashlán, who farmed fifty-five acres in the vicinity of Naharía. Thus it was that Abbas was brought up as an Egyptian rather than a Sudanese. On his death in 1930, Abbas left nine acres, which were divided between his widow and four sons. One of his sons, Hamed Abbas Naguib, served under my command as an ordnance sergeant at Gaza and Rafa; his brother, Abd el Latíf Naguib, was an ordnance corporal in Me'adi, a suburb of Cairo.

My father married again soon after returning to Sudan in 1900. My mother, his second wife, was Zahra Mohammed

Osman, an orphaned daughter of an Egyptian officer who was killed in the siege of Khartum two hours before the death of General Gordon. Her family came from Mehalla el Kobra, now a textile town, which is not far from Naharía. Lieutenant Colonel Mohammed Osman, my maternal grandfather, was an acting brigadier at the time of his death in 1885. Three of his brothers, who were also officers, were killed in the same massacre. My father asked Zahra's mother, whom he assumed to be her legal guardian, for permission to take her as his wife. To his surprise, my grandmother refused. She reminded him that proposals of marriage, according to Moslem etiquette, should be addressed to the senior male of the household. My father apologetically explained that he was unaware of the senior male's identity. As things turned out, he was none other than Lieutenant Abd el Wahab Osman, whom my father had known when they were both cadets at the Egyptian Military Academy. Abd el Wahab, who was still in Cairo, was Zahra's eldest brother. When my father wrote to him to ask for his sister's hand, he cordially consented, and my father married my mother a few weeks later.

I was the first of their nine children. The second was my brother Ali, who also became a general, and who, as I write, is now the Egyptian ambassador to Syria. Then came my six sisters—Dawlat, Zakía, Sennía, Hamida, Nemmat, and Naguía— and finally my brother Mahmúd, who is fourteen years my junior. Zakía and Nemmat have since died. All of my other sisters are married. Two of them, Sennía and Hamida, live in Sudan, where their husbands are employed in the civil service. Naguía, a pediatrician, is employed in the Child Welfare Division of the Egyptian Public Health Department. She is the author of a textbook on the care and feeding of infants. In 1953 she became the wife of Colonel Abd el Fatáh Gahber, a prison director, who was once my deputy in the Frontier Corps. Mahmúd, who is now studying for his doctorate, is an assistant professor of veterinary medicine at the University of Cairo.

II

Most of my childhood was spent in Wadi Halfa, near the Egyptian border, where my father was employed as a prison director until 1906, and where Ali and I attended school for several years thereafter. In 1906 my father was transferred to Wad Médani on the Blue Nile about a hundred miles above Khartum. A year later he was transferred to Singa, about seventy miles above Wad Médani, and in 1908 he was promoted to the rank of captain and appointed *ma'amúr,* or district commissioner, of Abu Ne'ama, about fifty miles above Singa. Two years later he was transferred back to Wadi Halfa and then, in 1912, he was transferred back to Wad Médani.

The work of a district commissioner in Sudan in the early years of the twentieth century was not very different from that of a Texas ranger in the late years of the nineteenth century. Much of my father's time was spent on horseback chasing bandits, smugglers, and cattle thieves.

Abu Ne'ama, which literally means "Father of Ostriches," was then a center of the feather trade. We kept six ostriches as pets, I remember, until the day one of them swallowed my mother's keys. Ostriches, like goats and chickens, will eat almost anything. We also kept a grivet monkey with a long tail and a sad triangular face. Once the monkey leaped from the top of a water jar onto the breast of one of the ostriches. I could never decide which was the more frightened of the two. The ostrich ran around in circles, squawking, until the monkey fell to the ground. While the monkey lay there whimpering like a newborn baby, the ostrich hid its head behind a basket in the corner.

The valley of the Blue Nile was full of game, and the walls of our houses in Wad Médani, Singa, and Abu Ne'ama were covered with the heads of the gazelles, gnus, buffaloes, and other animals that my father had shot. There were elephant tusks, too, and leopard and lion skins on the floor, and on one wall was the head of a rhinoceros that had chased my father up a tree. The rhino was killed by a member of the party that was sent to my father's rescue.

At night we could hear the cry of hyenas and the cough of leopards and occasionally the roar of a lion. During our summer vacations, as Ali and I grew older and learned how to handle guns, we often shot at crocodiles for practice from in front of our house, which overlooked the Blue Nile. Sometimes, on Fridays, after saying our Sabbath prayers at the local mosque, my father would take Ali and me across the river in a rowboat to hunt wild doves on the other side. Once, while looking for doves, we encountered a striped hyena, which I was allowed to shoot. Hyenas are reputed to be cowardly creatures, but I can testify from personal experience that they are occasionally aggressive. The only other hyena I ever shot was of the more common spotted variety. I was a second lieutenant at the time, in command of an infantry company working on the Sudan Railways below Khartum. The hyena attacked me at night a half mile down the track from where my men were working.

My father, who was an amateur gardener, did his best to inculcate in us a love for growing things. He succeeded, but only up to a point. For my part, I was always more interested in experimentation than I was in cultivation. Once, before returning to school in Wadi Halfa, I planted some strange seeds in my father's garden. He expressed his annoyance with me in one of his letters after scores of tabaldi seedlings had sprouted up in the midst of his cabbages and sunflowers. The tabaldi, or baobab, is the largest and fattest tree in East Africa. It bears a large green velvety fruit the size of a papaya, the seeds of which have a citrus flavor and are supposed to be good for curing fevers and purifying water.

Our houses in Singa and Abu Ne'ama were mud-and-wattle huts with thatched roofs. In Wad Médani, where the climate was drier, we lived in a one-story, mud-brick structure in the form of a hollow cube. Its flat roof was made of reed matting supported by beams and covered with layers of mud, dung, and straw. Ali and I found it an ideal place for playing chess and other games, of all of which my mother strongly disapproved. My father, who played chess himself, was prepared to distinguish between such a game of skill and the games of chance forbidden to Moslems by the Koran. My mother, on the other hand, believed that all games were gambling games and that even to play a game like marbles was a sin. Ali and I, like most boys everywhere, I suppose, when faced with such parental prohibitions, continued to play our games in secret. We liked chess better than marbles even though we never had a proper chess set. We used to make our chessmen out of mud, which we mixed in the patio and carried up to the roof when my mother wasn't looking. Our chessboard was simply a crosshatched piece of wrapping paper.

Every year before the rainy season it was necessary, at Wad Médani, to spread a fresh layer of mud, straw, and dung over the roof in order to make it waterproof. Once the roof had been thus prepared, Ali and I were forbidden access to it until after the rains. Here again we were often disobedient. One year, I remember, I sneaked up to the roof to have a look at it immediately after the fresh layer of paste had been applied. It looked and smelled so fertile that I couldn't resist the temptation to sprinkle some of my father's seeds on it to see what would happen. My father was furious when the rains came and he discovered what I had done. Radishes were sprouting all over the roof, which their roots had perforated in so many places that it was leaking like a filter.

In arid Wadi Halfa, where we lived in the same sort of mudbrick house, I once built myself a miniature fortress in the patio. It consisted of a deep hole surrounded by a wall of dried mud and sand. Whenever I could, I inserted firecrackers, which were supposed to be cannons, in the crenelations that I had cut into the top of the wall. Then I would climb inside and shoot off the firecrackers at whoever entered the patio.

Usually I was a general, but sometimes I was an admiral, too, because the fortress also served as a naval base. Among the other objects that I liked to secrete inside were a couple of toy German locomotives and several destroyers—or at least I thought of them as destroyers; actually they were old door locks.

I was so proud of my fortress that one day, to demonstrate the strength of its walls, I placed a large copper tray on top of it and invited a friend of my mother's, a very fat woman, to sit on the tray. Having found that the fortress would withstand her weight, I decided to test it further by sitting on top of the tray myself with one of my sisters inside. I gave her such a fright that my mother, as punishment, compelled me to destroy the fortress and never allowed me to build another.

III

In 1913, after my father had been transferred back to Wad Médani, I entered Gordon College in Khartum.

My education had begun with a thorough study of the Koran, which has never failed to give me strength in my hours of need. The Koran affects different people in different ways. Its chief effect on me has usually been to convert my pessimism into optimism, which I consider the prerequisite to success. In Palestine I read the Koran for half an hour every day. As a boy I used to read it in preparing for my examinations. It helped me to obtain high marks if only because it filled me with self-confidence. Unlike some people, I have never read the Koran merely in the hope that it would bring me luck. I have read it, instead, in order to exalt my spirit and also to increase my command of the Arabic language. Luck, I have found, usually abandons those whose spirits are low; by the same token, it usually accompanies those whose spirits are high.

My father wanted me to be a good student, and I seldom disappointed him. Once, after I had come home from Wadi Halfa with a bad report card, he took me aside and gave me a lecture that I have never forgotten.

"I always tried to be the first in my class," he said. "I want you to do the same. I'll forgive you anything if you do your best; I'll forgive you nothing if you don't."

My father was opposed to my studying after midnight, but I often studied all night long, especially before examinations. At midnight he would turn off the gasoline lanterns and make me go to bed, examination or no, but, if it was the right time of month,

I would sneak up to the roof of our house to continue studying by the light of the moon.

Before leaving Wad Médani, I performed my *shatara,* or trial by fire, which consisted of branding the left forearm without displaying any signs of fear or pain. I used a red-hot nail for the purpose, but many Sudanese, and especially those in the more primitive regions, used burning cornstalks filled with water. As an Egyptian and the son of the district commissioner, I was not expected, in theory, to perform the rite, although in practice I knew that I would have been considered a coward if I failed to do what every young Sudanese was expected to do as a matter of course. It was a cruel custom, perhaps, but one of which I am inclined to approve. I think it is a good thing for boys to learn as soon as possible that life, among other things, is an ordeal to be suffered without flinching.

Of the two of us, I was the better student and Ali the better sportsman. We had both wanted to be soldiers for as long as either of us could remember, although my father wanted only one of us to follow in his footsteps. The Egyptian Army, he said, was not all that it was supposed to be. It was not really an army at all, but rather an auxiliary corps in which Egyptians were expected to take orders from the British. Even he, who called himself an Egyptian officer, was merely a servant of the British who ruled Egypt from behind the scenes as surely as they ruled Sudan from the center of the stage. Since I was the better student, it would be better for Ali to be the officer and for me to be a lawyer or an engineer. I could do more for my country in civilian clothes, he thought, than I could ever do for it in uniform.

As a student at Gordon College, which was then but a technological high school, I was given many opportunities to ponder the wisdom of my father's remarks.[1] One of his friends was Ibrahim Orabi, a government clerk at Wad Médani. Orabi was a son of Ahmed Orabi, the colonel who had led the abortive revolt of 1882. Ahmed Orabi, in trying to free Egypt, had succeeded only in precipitating the British occupation. His death sentence was commuted to life imprisonment in Ceylon, and in 1901, a broken old man, he was pardoned and allowed to return to Egypt on condition that he keep out of politics. His son agreed with my father that I would do well to abandon my military ambitions.

"You'll never get anywhere," he warned me, "because you'll never be anything more than an overseer for the British."

Gordon College offered courses leading to three different government careers—teacher, magistrate, and engineer. Since it was necessary to elect one or another of these courses in order to remain in school, I tentatively elected to become an engineer, even though I still hoped to become a soldier. I chose the engineering course because my father believed it would offer me the best chance of winning a scholarship at a British university. But the warden of Gordon College, M. F. Simpson, rejected my application.

"You're an Egyptian," he explained, "and you'll have to be a teacher. The engineering course is for Sudanese only."

One of my own teachers, N. R. Udal, who was later to become the warden, put the matter even more bluntly.

"The purpose of Gordon College," he said, "is to train Sudanese for government careers. It is not intended to be a school for Egyptians. If we allow you to study here it is only because your father is a civil servant."

Such remarks were not calculated to make me an obedient student. Flogging was the customary punishment at Gordon Col-

[1]In 1952 Gordon College became the University College of Khartum.

lege in those days as I believe it was at every British high school. I was flogged three times by an English teacher alone. Once, during a lesson, he chose to dictate a passage from a book in which it was stated that Egypt was governed by the British. Without thinking, I leaped to my feet and said, "No, sir, Egypt is not governed by the British. Egypt is merely occupied by the British." The teacher warned me that he would flog me if I said another word, but I was so excited that I failed to heed his warning. He took me to the warden, explained what I had done, and was duly authorized to give me ten lashes with the heavy strap that was kept in the warden's office.

The same teacher flogged me again when he caught me writing a speech entitled "The Civilization of Egypt and Sudan." Anything connected with Egypt's national claims was a forbidden topic at Gordon College.

A year later, as he was returning our notebooks at the end of the term, the teacher read aloud what he had written on the cover of mine: "Composition excellent; writing awful." With that, he tossed my book out of the open window beside his desk and then ordered me to retrieve it. When I refused to do so, he administered another ten lashes with the warden's strap.

Napoleon was my first hero. At Wad Médani, I remember, I slept on the floor instead of in bed because I had read in a book that Napoleon had done the same. I have eaten brown bread all my life for the same reason. Gradually, though, my interest in Napoleon waned as my interest in Mustafa Kamel, the founder of the Egyptian Nationalist Party, increased. Among the forbidden books I read during my last year as a primary student at Wad Médani was *The Eastern Question*, Kamel's nine-volume study of the struggle between Britain, France, and Russia to dominate the dying Ottoman Empire, of which Egypt, in theory, was still a part.

I was also an avid reader of *Politics Illustrated,* a sensational magazine published by Ahmed Zaki, a former Egyptian Army officer. One of its covers, I remember, depicted Egypt as a scorpion wearing a *tarbúsh;* another depicted Moslem India as a cobra wearing a turban. Both were intent on biting John Bull in the seat of his pants. It was heady reading for a youngster, I admit, and not at all the fare that my British teachers would have recommended. But it was the sort of thing that appealed to young Egyptians on the eve of the First World War—a war that was to free the Arab peoples from Turkish bondage only to tie them against their will to the empires of the British and the French.

In later years I became a follower of Sa'ad Zaghlul, the founder of the Wafd, or Delegation, as his party was called, who forced the British to recognize Egypt's nominal sovereignty under King Fuad. Today, aside from the Prophet Mohammed, the historical figures I most admire are Mohandas Gandhi, the liberator of India, and Sun Yat-sen, the father of the Chinese Republic. In some ways, I also admire Mustafa Kemál Atatürk. As I shall explain in a later chapter, however, the problems of Egypt are so different from those of Turkey that I could not be an "Egyptian Atatürk" even if I had the desire and the ruthless character necessary to be one.

IV

On the afternoon of June 9, 1914, I was sitting in the dormitory at Gordon College, preparing for my examinations. Suddenly the mental image of my father began to dominate my thoughts. I felt that he was trying to tell me something of the utmost importance, but it was something that I was unable to understand. I grew so depressed that I put my books aside and took up the mouth organ that I was learning how to play. Without thinking, I began to play the Egyptian Army's funeral march, and, to my surprise, I played it better than anything that I had yet attempted. But I was not elated. On the contrary, I was so disconsolate that I stood up and began to walk around the dormitory. I took off my belt and slung it over my shoulder like a bandolier. I then stood before a mirror, staring at myself in silence. Presently tears began to roll down my cheeks. Some of my classmates laughed at me; others stared at me in alarm.

After supper I went to the study hall and again attempted to prepare for my examinations. As the clock struck nine, I stood up and ripped the sleeves from my *galabia,* the cotton robe that most of us wore on informal occasions instead of our hot and expensive Western clothing. One of the teachers who was present asked me if I was going mad. I fled from the study hall in tears.

The next morning, after a sleepless night, I was sitting in the garden waiting for the examinations to begin. Suddenly I stood up, took off my *tarbúsh,* and began to stamp it into the ground as though it were the cause of my depression.

A few minutes later my history teacher, S. Hillelson, brought one of the warden's secretaries to see me. The secretary began to tell me how we must all be prepared to face the tragedies of life, but I cut him short, for I had finally understood.

"What you're trying to tell me," I said, "is that my father is dead."

The secretary nodded. My father had died in the Khartum hospital at ten minutes past nine the night before, just ten minutes after I had ripped the sleeves from my *galabia.* I hope it will not seem superstitious if I say that I have always considered my strange behavior on that occasion a clear example of extra-sensory perception. No one had told me that my father was even ill. He had died of peritonitis resulting from an inflamed appendix that had burst while he was chasing some escaping bandits. By the time he reached the hospital it was already too late to save his life, which was why I had not been taken to see him. Had he lived a few weeks longer he would have died a major rather than a captain, for his promotion had already been approved.

Mr. Hillelson offered to excuse me from my history examination, but I insisted on taking it, and, in spite of my sorrow, I managed to pass it with a high mark. Later I went to the morgue to see my father's body. I removed the shroud with which he was covered and kissed his forehead, which was surprisingly cold, although the day was very hot. I no longer felt depressed. I was merely worried now about how the rest of us were going to face the future. So far as I knew from what my mother had told me, I was my father's eldest son, and as such would be responsible for my family's welfare even though I was only fifteen, as I thought at the time, or thirteen, as I now believe.

My father left an estate consisting of twelve and a half acres of farmland in the vicinity of Naharía. The estate was divided according to Islamic law. One eighth, or 12.5 per cent, went to my mother as his widow; one seventh of the remainder, or 12.5 per cent, to each of his four sons; and one fourteenth, or 6.25 per cent, to each of his daughters. This meant that my mother and my brothers and I, including Abbas and Mahmúd (who was then only six months old), each inherited a little over an acre and a half, while my sisters each inherited a little over three quarters of an acre.

My mother also received a lump-sum payment of LE 196 for the care of her nine children, plus a monthly widow's pension from the Egyptian Government of LE 2.03 per month. The Egyptian pound in those days was worth about $5.00—almost twice its present value of $2.87.

Even though Abbas turned out to be my father's eldest son, I was obliged, as I had expected, to act as the senior male of our household. For the next fourteen years, until my mother's death in 1928, I was seldom free of financial worries. The family continued to live in Wad Médani while Ali and I continued our studies at Gordon College. The Civil Servants' Club paid the rent on our house until I was able to pay it myself out of my earnings as an officer.

Now that my father was dead, I was more determined than ever to become a soldier. My teachers were equally determined that I should become a clerk. Including Ali, who had entered Gordon College in the autumn of 1914, there were six of us Egyptian students who had elected the teaching course. Because of our national feelings, however, it was decided not to permit us to teach school in Sudan. We were accordingly required to study typing and to work as apprentices during our vacations in one or another of the government offices in Khartum. Our teachers apparently hoped that we would resign ourselves to the inevitable as soon as we had grown accustomed to bureaucratic life.

But I had another plan. During my third vacation I worked as an apprentice clerk in the Wellcome Tropical Research Laboratories. By saving every piaster of my wages, I was able to accumulate, with my other savings, a total of LE 9, and with these I fled to Cairo in January 1917.

Since I was a truant, and not yet sixteen at the time, I was afraid of being arrested at the Egyptian border. I disguised myself as a Sudanese servant and traveled as far as Atbara in the company of Mohammed Saleh Behairi, a Sudanese teacher who had graduated from Gordon College the year before. From Atbara I traveled fourth class as far as Halfa Camp, where I alighted from the train and walked into Wadi Halfa in the midst of a group of tribesmen. To avoid detection by the immigration authorities, I tarried in the market place until the steamer to Shellal was ready to leave. In the confusion attending the raising of the gangplank I was able to slip aboard unnoticed. I sneaked ashore at the first landing above Shellal, the Egyptian railhead, where I later boarded the narrow-gauge train for Asswan just as it was leaving the station. In Asswan, since I was no longer in danger of being detected, I changed into my Western clothes and bought a third-class ticket on the standard-gauge train to Cairo.

In Cairo I lived with Captain Mohammed es Saíd Samaha, a friend of my father's, who did what he could to help me to enter the Egyptian Military Academy. Unfortunately the academic term had already begun, and Captain Samaha was told that no more applications could be considered until the opening of the second term in April. Since I was unable to wait that long, I obtained an audience with Sultan Hussein, who promised to do what he could to help me. I also obtained an audience with General Wingate, the British High Commissioner. Wingate, who remembered both my father and my uncle Abd el Wahab, instructed General Herbert, the commandant of the Military Academy, to admit me in the second term, provided I was found to be "fit for duty."

I then returned to Khartum and re-entered Gordon College. Mr. Simpson, the warden, advised me to give up my attempt to enter the Military Academy and to resign myself to being a government clerk in Sudan. In March, however, I received a telegram from General Herbert, who ordered me to report for my physical examination in Cairo on April 1. Again I returned to

Cairo, and this time a friend of Captain Samaha's was waiting for me in the station. He handed me the new suit of Western clothes that Samaha had bought for me in answer to the telegram I had sent him from Shellal. I changed into my new suit in the men's room and took a streetcar to the Military Academy. General Herbert was inspecting the other would-be cadets when I arrived. I waited until he had finished his inspection and then presented myself, hoping against hope that he would fail to notice how small I was. After looking me over from head to foot he shook his head.

"I'm sorry," he said, "but I'm afraid you're too small to be a cadet."

I was then only five feet three. The regulations, I knew, required all cadets to be at least five feet four in height. I was on the verge of tears, but I reminded Herbert with the best grace I could that I was only sixteen. My father, I added, had also been small when he was my age but he had finally achieved the proper height.

Herbert turned to his chief medical officer, a Colonel Carroll, who was standing beside him.

"What do you think?" he said, nodding in my direction.

"I think he'll grow," said Carroll. "Let's give him a chance."

Herbert finally agreed to admit me to the academy on condition that I grow to be five feet four before I graduated.

In Khartum I had bought a patented stretching machine, and for months I had stretched and stretched, to the intense amusement of my classmates at Gordon College. Now I joined the track team and ran, jumped, and hurdled every afternoon. I also took up fencing and gymnastics in the hope that one form of exercise or another would help to increase my height. The best I could do before I graduated from the academy was five feet three and a half, but General Herbert was good enough to overlook the last half inch. I eventually grew to be five feet eight, and today, at an age when most of my contemporaries have grown rather fat, I am still so slender that I look taller than I really am. Although I have never dieted, except during Ramadan, the Moslem equivalent of Lent, I have never been a heavy eater and my weight has yet to exceed 160 pounds. My habit of smoking crushed Tuscan cigars in my pipe, I think, has tended to limit my appetite.

V

Although I failed to graduate from Gordon College, my education was so much better than that of most of my classmates that I completed my two-and-a-half-year course at the Military Academy in eleven months. There were five classes, each divided into two terms of three months each. Twenty-four hours after entering the academy, I was promoted from the fifth to the fourth class. Ten weeks later, after obtaining the highest marks in the fourth class, I was promoted to the third. The First World War was then in progress, and officers were so badly needed that the nine best students in the second class were given their commissions immediately. I was one of the six best in the third class who were advanced to the second to take their places. In January 1918, I passed my examinations with an average of 97.7. A month later, because of another shortage of officers, I was graduated as a second lieutenant and assigned to the 17th Egyptian Infantry Battalion in Sudan.

Although I was happier at the Military Academy than I had ever been at Gordon College, I would have been happier still if

I had not been graduated in such a hurry. I was given no time to perfect either my horsemanship or my marksmanship. Although I was able to do so later, in my spare time, I would have preferred to do so at the academy, as Ali was able to do. Above all I had wanted to be the sergeant major of my class and to be given a chance to win the engraved sword and other honors to which my high marks entitled me but which, for lack of time, I failed to receive. I was so disappointed that I wept on the day of my graduation.

"Don't worry," said Herbert. "You'll have plenty of time to win distinction later on. The important thing now is to learn to be a good officer. I've graduated you ahead of your class because I think you're destined to succeed. I want you to have all the seniority you can get. You'll need it if you ever try to become a general."

Herbert was right. My seniority would prove to be more important than any honors I might have won at the academy. Even so, I was acutely embarrassed the day Abdullah Khalil invited me to go hunting with him near Khartum. Abdullah was to become not only the first native brigadier in the Sudan Defense Force but also the first president of his country's legislative assembly. He was then a first lieutenant and already a famous marksman. On our hunting trip he kindly offered to let me use his new automatic shotgun, a .303. I was terrified the first time I fired the gun for fear of missing my target. With a trembling hand, I raised the gun and fired it at an ibis in a nearby field. The bird fell as if in answer to the silent prayer I had uttered as I raised Abdullah's gun.

"You're very accurate," Abdullah said in English.

For the first time in my life I understood what "accurate" meant. It was a word that I had often used when speaking English, but until that moment I had thought that it meant "correct" or "normal" rather than "exact." Although I speak English far better than any other foreign language, having learned it as a child, I have never been sure of the exact meanings of many English words. Even today I am frequently surprised to discover that certain words have different meanings from those that I had been giving them. I am therefore inclined to be tolerant of international misunderstandings, for I know from personal experience how difficult it is to render one's meaning exactly in a foreign language.

The 17th Battalion was encamped at Wad Bánnaga, just below Khartum. For the first few months I had so little to do that I began to study French. Later I studied Italian and German, and as late as 1949, as I was recovering from the wounds I received in Palestine, I began to study Hebrew. I was so disturbed by our lack of translators during the war that one of the first things I did after taking office in 1952 was to add Hebrew to the list of languages taught at the Military Academy and at the universities of Cairo and Alexandria.

My first military assignment in Sudan was not military at all. I was attached to an infantry company whose task was to move a railway track that was threatened by the rising waters of the Nile. Our soldiers were each required to move six cubic yards of earth per day. They were paid nothing for the first three yards and a piaster each for the fourth, fifth, and sixth, provided they maintained their daily quota. It was forced labor disguised as military service. For months we broke rock and built embankments at a fraction of what it would have cost the Sudan Railways if a private contractor had been employed to do the job. I often thought of Ibrahim Orabi and his prediction, which seemed to be coming true, that I would never be anything more than an overseer for the British. I began to wonder if my father had not been right and if I would not have done better to become a lawyer or an engineer. I accordingly bought some books and began to study for my baccalaureate in order to be free to study law or engineering later on.

In 1919, I was transferred to a Sudanese cavalry squadron that was garrisoned at Shendi, between Khartum and Atbara. Ali, who had just graduated from the Military Academy, was attached to the same squadron. It was at Shendi that I finally perfected my horsemanship and learned how to play a passable game of polo. But I found it impossible to get along with my British superiors at Shendi, and I was eventually transferred back to the 17th Egyptian Infantry.

In the meantime Sa'ad Zaghlul and several other Egyptian nationalist leaders had been banished to Malta. In 1918, following the armistice, Zaghlul had requested permission to lead a delegation (wafd) to Paris to lay Egypt's claim to independence before the Peace Conference. In spite of Wingate's favorable recommendation, and in spite of the fact that Syria, Hejaz (now part of Saudi Arabia), and even Cyprus were sending delegations to Paris, the British Government refused Zaghlul's request. It refused even to receive an Egyptian delegation in London. The result was the abortive revolt of 1919. Bloody rioting occurred all over Egypt and in some parts of Sudan. Zaghlul and his principal lieutenants were arrested and Wingate was replaced as High Commissioner by Viscount Allenby. Lord Milner was later sent to Egypt to investigate the causes of the riots and eventually, at Allenby's insistence, Zaghlul was released and the Wafd was allowed to function as a political party. In 1922 the British grudgingly recognized Egypt's nominal independence. Fuad, who had succeeded Hussein as our Sultan, now became our King.

It was because of these events and my own bitter experiences with the British that I joined the White Banner in 1923. I had been sent to Cairo in 1921 to be trained as a police officer, but I so disliked the work that I was transferred at my own request to the 13th Sudanese Infantry Battalion in the province of Bahr el Ghazal, on the border of Belgian Congo. I took advantage of my stay in Cairo, however, to pass my examinations for the high school diploma that I had failed to obtain in Khartum. Now I was sent to Malakal, the capital of the province of the Upper Nile, to take a training course in the use of modern machine guns. Once again I found myself in difficulties with the British. The chief instructor, a Colonel Knapp, at first refused to admit me to the training course on the ground that it was intended for Sudanese and not for Egyptians. But I stood up for my rights as an officer in an Army in which Egyptians, Sudanese, and Britons were supposed to be on an equal footing, and I was finally allowed to take the course after Knapp had consulted his superiors in Khartum. In the end he commended me as the best of all his students.

Before long I was recalled to Cairo to impart my knowledge of machine guns to the Royal Guards. In the meantime I had completed my studies for my baccalaureate, which I obtained in Cairo in 1924. In the same year I also became a first lieutenant. But I was advancing so slowly and was so unhappy as a member of the Royal Guards that I began to study law in my spare time with the thought of resigning my commission and becoming an attorney and, possibly, a politician.

VI

As a junior officer I saw very little of King Fuad, though he occasionally condescended to address me through his military aide. Fuad, unlike Faruk, had never bothered to perfect his Arabic. He preferred to speak Turkish in private and French in public. I now understand why my father habitually referred to the royal family as "those Turks" or "those Albanians." Fuad was a foreigner to Egypt. Once, when it was suggested that he refer to himself as the King of Sudan as well as Egypt, he declined for fear of annoying the British. He was content, he said, to be the *"Umda* of Abdín." By that he meant that he was content to play the role that the British had assigned to him as the first King of modern Egypt—namely, to preside over the royal palace and nothing more.

Before he ascended the throne, Fuad had been an impoverished playboy who owed money to everyone. Once he became King, however, he devoted himself to saving as much money as he could. He never spent a piaster if he could possibly avoid it. He gave nothing to charity, except on formal occasions, and to my knowledge he once ordered the flogging of a Royal Guard who had picked some dates from one of the palm trees in the garden of Bustan Palace. In 1925, to save money, Fuad even abolished the free rations that had long been one of the perquisites of the officers of the Royal Guards.

Queen Nazli, on the other hand, was a kindly person in spite of her many foibles. Once, I remember, my mother and two of my sisters went to call on the Queen by mistake. The wives and womenfolk of the Royal Guards had been invited to a tea party on the occasion of the opening of Parliament. My mother and sisters, instead of going to the Royal Guards' barracks, where they should have gone, went to Abdín Palace itself, where they were admitted to the *haramlik,* the quarters reserved for the Queen and her ladies in waiting. They were received by Rizah Aga, a tremendous Ethiopian, who was Fuad's chief eunuch (an office that Faruk happily abolished). Rizah Aga ushered them into the presence of the Queen, who did her best to put them at their ease. They left as soon as they could, but not before Nazli had presented them with gifts and announced that she would repay their visit.

That night my mother tearfully expressed the fear that I would be dismissed from the Royal Guards in consequence of her *faux pas.* For my part, I was afraid only of embarrassing the Queen if she called at our modest house, which was in one of the less fashionable sections of Cairo. My mother had used one of my visiting cards to identify herself, and I assumed that the Queen had received her in the mistaken impression that she was related to a certain Mohammed Naguib who happened to be a pasha. A few days later a police officer attached to the palace called at our house to announce the impending arrival of some of the Queen's ladies in waiting. I explained to the officer that it was all a mistake and begged him to tender our apologies to the Queen. He must have done so, for her ladies in waiting never appeared.

I was dismissed from the Royal Guards soon afterward, but not because of the incident that I have just described. Two Sudanese friends of mine, Ahmed Hassan Mattar and Arafat Mohammed Abdullah, both of whom were fellow members of the White Banner, had been arrested on suspicion of complicity in the assassination of General Sir Lee Stack, the Governor General of Sudan and the Commander in Chief of the Egyptian Army. General Stack had been shot and mortally wounded in Cairo on November 19, 1924. Three days later Viscount Allenby issued an ultimatum that few Egyptians of my age have either forgotten or forgiven.

Allenby not only demanded an apology and the payment of a fine amounting to £500,000 (then about $2,430,000); he also demanded the prohibition of political demonstrations; the retention of the British financial, judicial, and other advisers whom the Egyptian Government had decided to dismiss; and the withdrawal from Sudan, which would henceforth have its own private Defense Force, of all Egyptian troops. As a final punishment, Allenby abolished the restrictions on irrigation that had hitherto been applied to the Gezira area above Khartum. Henceforth, instead of being allowed to draw only enough water from the White Nile to irrigate 300,000 acres, the British-controlled Gezira Project would be free to draw all the water it could use, regardless of the needs of farmers in Lower Egypt.

Like most Egyptians, I sincerely regretted Stack's assassination, and I was thoroughly in favor of punishing everyone who was in any way responsible for the crime. At the same time I resented Allenby's ultimatum, for I felt that he had used the incident as a pretext for exacting concessions that he had no right to demand. I was so indignant, in fact, when I learned that my friends had been arrested, that I went to call on them at the Bab el Khalk Prison. I was sure they were innocent, but, though they were later acquitted, the mere fact that I had visited them in my Royal Guards uniform aroused so much suspicion that I was confined to my quarters when I returned to Abdín Palace.

Ali, who was also a member of the Royal Guards at the time, telephoned to ask me what had happened. I was afraid to tell him over the telephone, but I later sent a mutual friend to ask him to hide my personal papers. I was afraid of being arrested myself, but my only punishment in the end was to be dismissed from the Royal Guards.

As the Koran says, "It may be that you dislike a thing while it is good for you, and it may be that you love a thing while it is evil for you; and Allah knows while you know not." Although I was bitter at being ousted from the Royal Guards, my dismissal turned out to be a blessing in disguise. I was soon attached to the 8th Infantry Battalion, which was then garrisoned in Me'adi. I was given so little to do that I was able to resume my studies and obtain my law degree in 1927. In that year I was married for the first time. Two years later I obtained my master's degree in political economy, and in 1931, the year in which my daughter Samiha was born, I obtained my master's degree in private law. I was on the point of resigning from the Army when I was unexpectedly promoted to the rank of captain. My promotion so elated me that I decided to remain in the Army instead of trying to start a private law practice at the age of thirty. I later changed my mind again and began to study for my doctorate with the thought of becoming a professor of political economy. But from then on I had so little time to spare that I was unable to produce an acceptable thesis. The best of the five theses I prepared, "The Human Aspects of the Army and Its Welfare," eventually served as the basis of a course of lectures that I delivered at the Senior Officers' School.

VII

One of the happiest periods of my life began in May 1934, when I was transferred to the Frontier Corps. In August of that

year, forty days after divorcing my first wife, I married Aisha
Labíb. Like my father's second wife, my mother, Aisha was an
orphaned daughter of a lieutenant colonel of infantry. Aisha lived
with her widowed mother, a brother, and three sisters in a large
house in Helmíet el Zeitún, the same suburb of Cairo in which we
were to settle after the Palestinian War.

"I hope you understand our financial situation," she said, after
I had obtained her brother's permission to take her as my wife.
"We used to have a large income but now all we have is debts."

I chided her jokingly for cutting off my line of retreat.

"If I don't marry you now," I said, "it will look as if I were
interested only in your money."

Actually her whole family was living on an income of LE 80
(then about $390) a month. Hassan Kashef Nur ed Din, her
maternal grandfather, had owned 512 acres of farmland near
Beni Mazar in Lower Egypt. Before his death he had converted
his estate into a private trust fund to be administered according to
Islamic law by the Ministry of Wakfs. The executors appointed by
the ministry had so mismanaged the estate that his heirs owed LE
26,000 (then about $125,000), which was almost half as much
as the land was worth. After the Revolution the antiquated system
of administering private *wakfs,* or trust funds, was abolished.
Nur ed Din's estate was liquidated, and, after the payment of
debts and taxes, Aisha inherited seventy acres, the income from
which, LE 1400 (now worth about $4000), amounts to almost
half my salary as the President of Egypt. But I have never used
any of my wife's income, even on clothing for our sons, for I
have always felt that the bulk of such money rightfully belongs
to the *fellahín.*

During the first year of our marriage we lived at El Arísh, on
the Mediterranean coast of Sinai, but I was seldom at home for

very long. Most of my time was spent in the desert chasing smugglers. If my father's duty as a district commissioner in Sudan was comparable to that of a Texas ranger, my own duty as a captain in the Frontier Corps was comparable to that of an internal revenue agent before the repeal of prohibition in the United States. The drug traffic is a serious problem in every country, but it is far more serious in the Moslem East than it is in the Christian West, where the drinking of alcohol is a commoner vice than the smoking of hashish, or marihuana, the cheapest and therefore the commonest of the drugs to which non-drinking Moslems are addicted. Since the Revolution we have increased the penalty for illegal possession of drugs to life imprisonment, but even today it is no easy matter to obtain a conviction, for the law still provides, as it must, that the accused be caught with the drugs in his actual possession.

One of my first successes as a captain in the Frontier Corps was the capture of Sallam Khader Abu Fadel, one of the most dangerous of the smugglers then operating in the Eastern Desert. Unfortunately Abu Fadel was able to unload his camels and throw his bales of hashish into the sea before I caught him. It was not until several years later that he was finally caught with the evidence in his possession and sentenced to a long term in prison.

On another occasion I led a chase that resulted in the capture of five smugglers and the seizure of 9140 bundles of hashish. (I have never forgotten the number because the first three figures corresponded with the last three figures of the year in which the First World War began.) With the help of an elderly tracker named Doma Awad, I overtook the five smugglers as they were leading four camels laden with hashish up the Wadi el Gedi toward Missbah Pass. They retreated up a boulder-strewn hill and opened fire on us before we could close in on them. Our only alternative was to take cover and return their fire until the issue was resolved. I exposed my cap and ordered Doma to expose his turban in the hope of giving the impression that we were four instead of two. But the smugglers were undeceived, and presently they began to advance down the hill, firing five shots at us for every shot that we could fire at them.

Inasmuch as I was armed only with a revolver, and Doma was showing signs of fright, I seized his rifle to prevent him from escaping. Fortunately I killed one of our five opponents with a lucky shot, whereupon Doma recovered his courage and begged me to return his rifle, which I did. He wounded one of the four remaining smugglers just as the sun was setting. The others, instead of trying to hold out until darkness fell, decided to surrender just as another patrol approached us from the opposite direction.

A month or two later Doma and I set out after another band of smugglers. This time the chase lasted for fourteen days. The smugglers kept zigzagging back and forth from one side of a sandy ridge to the other in the hope that the wind would obliterate their tracks. Within a few days we and our camels were approaching exhaustion. I had to fight with Doma to prevent him from drinking our last half bottle of water. We finally found a well, but the water it contained was so brackish that, after drinking it, we both came down with diarrhea. We might have died if we had not been found by a wandering goatherd, who sold us a skinful of milk and directed us to a more potable well. After filling our bottles we continued the chase, but before long the weaker of our two camels fell and refused to rise again. We left him behind and continued on foot, leading his stronger companion. On the ninth day we found the smugglers retreating before another patrol. Together we pursued them back and forth across the dunes and mountains until, on the fourteenth day, they chose to surrender rather than

die of exhaustion. We ourselves had eaten nothing for two days
except the gum from occasional thorn trees.

At lunch in Suez a few days later my good friend Shawki Abd
er Rahmán, who is now a major general, predicted that I would
be decorated for bravery. I was feeling rather sorry for myself
and predicted that I wouldn't. He suggested that we make it a bet,
and so we agreed that whoever lost would have to buy the other a
full-course meal at his first opportunity.

My next patrol was in the vicinity of St. Catherine's Monastery,
which lies at the foot of Geb el Mussa, or the Mount of Moses,
otherwise known as Mount Sinai. It was here, according to the
Book of Exodus, that Moses saw the Burning Bush. I was escorted
through the monastery by an Orthodox priest, an Arabic-speaking
Greek, who called my attention to an icon of the Virgin Mary. A
small silver hand had been affixed to the icon immediately above
the lamp that was burning in front of it. The hand, said the priest,
was in memory of a miraculous occurrence. The priest whose duty
it was to fill the lamp with oil each morning had once overslept.
Just as the lamp was going out he was awakened by an invisible
hand that slapped his face. He was so ashamed of himself that
he affixed the miniature hand to the icon in the hope of atoning
for his sloth.

The Virgin Mary is revered by Moslems as well as Christians.
Though we do not regard her as the mother of God, or even as
the mother of the son of God, we do regard her as the mother of
the Prophet Jesus, who was as close to God in his own way as the
Prophet Mohammed was in his. I was therefore glad to join the
priest in praying before her image.

On my return to Suez a few days later I learned from Abd er
Rahmán that I had indeed been decorated as he had bet me that
I would be. I had been decorated, moreover, on October 21, the

very day that I had prayed before the Virgin at St. Catherine's Monastery. I bought Abd er Rahmán the most sumptuous meal that either of us had eaten in weeks.

I enjoyed patrolling the desert as much as anything I have ever done. It was a hard and dangerous life, but it was full of compensations. It gave me a sense of physical and spiritual well-being such as I had never experienced before and have seldom experienced since.

Occasionally, on my patrols, I would be called upon to play the role of healer. The beduin of the desert, like primitive people everywhere, suffer from numerous chronic ailments that can be easily cured but seldom are because of their poverty and ignorance and their nomadic way of life. In my pack I carried a first-aid kit containing a supply of aspirin, eye lotion, unguents, astringents, and laxatives, as well as iodine, medicinal alcohol, and bandages. Whenever I visited a beduin camp I was usually called upon to treat one or more persons for sore eyes, stomach-ache, or infected wounds.

Once I was asked to treat a child who was suffering from insomnia. I couldn't very well refuse, and so, praying to God for His forgiveness, I gave the child an aspirin tablet, passed my hand before its eyes in the manner of a hypnotist, and murmured some meaningless incantations. The next time I encountered the same band of beduin I was greeted with cheers. The child, thanks (it was supposed) to my ministrations, was now sleeping normally.

My undeserved reputation as a healer spread to such an extent that hardly a day passed from then on without my being called upon to cure somebody of his ills. I was even asked to treat a woman with a swollen belly, which was a mark of great confidence, for desert Arabs are reluctant to let even genuine physicians examine their womenfolk for fear of their being dishonored.

I decided, after examining her, that the woman was suffering from a tumor of some sort and that an operation would be necessary. I sent her to the hospital in Suez, where one of the surgeons confirmed my amateur diagnosis and performed a successful operation. The end result of such attentions was that the beduin kept me informed of the movements of the smugglers I was seeking to arrest.

My greatest success as a healer resulted from the treatment I prescribed for a young husband who complained of impotence. I gave him half a dozen eggs, two cans of bully beef, and two of my four remaining laxative pills. I told him to take the pills as soon as he had consumed the rest of my prescription. I warned him that the pills would make his belly ache, but I also hinted that they would restore his powers if he only stopped worrying about his supposed loss of virility.

Eleven years later, when I was the deputy governor of Sinai, I returned to the same area to preside over a peace conference between two tribes that had been engaged in a long dispute over the use of certain grazing lands. One of the lesser shaikhs who was present suddenly prostrated himself before me. He then presented one of his sons—the result, he said, of the magic pills that I had given him eleven years before.

VIII

In 1935, following the Italian invasion of Ethiopia, I was transferred to the Western Desert to command a squadron of light cars. It was feared that the Italians, who were massing troops in Libya, might be tempted to invade Egypt if they were frustrated in Ethiopia. My squadron's task was to patrol the border south of Sollum. We operated in liaison with other Egyptian and British forces, among which were units of the 1st Essex Regiment and the 5th Northumberland Fusiliers. Both were then based at Mersa Matruh.

In 1936, after the Italians had conquered Ethiopia and had consequently ceased to threaten Egypt, I was reassigned to Cairo to serve as a deputy adjutant general under Brigadier Hassan Abd el Wahab. The year 1936 was one of the most eventful in the history of modern Egypt. King Fuad died in April and was succeeded by Faruk in May. In August, Egypt and Great Britain signed a twenty-year treaty of friendship and alliance.

The Treaty of 1936, as it came to be known, terminated the British occupation of all but a small portion of Egypt—the Suez Canal Zone, where a maximum of 10,000 soldiers, including 400 fliers, were to be based for the treaty's duration. The treaty also abolished the legal immunities and special privileges enjoyed by Britons and other foreigners in Egypt and the discriminatory restrictions to which Egyptians had been subjected in Sudan. It reduced the status of the British High Commissioner to that of an ambassador and established a British military mission to train and equip the Egyptian Army to the extent necessary to ensure the defense of Egypt without further assistance from the British Army except "in the event of war, imminent menace of war or apprehended international emergency." In such an event the King of Egypt was obliged to make available to the King and Emperor of Great Britain "all the facilities and assistance in his power, including the use of his ports, aerodromes and means of communication, [and] to take all the administrative and legislative measures, including the establishment of martial law and an effective censorship, necessary to render these facilities and assistance effective [sic]."

It was hardly an ideal treaty from the Egyptian point of view inasmuch as it authorized a limited British occupation for another twenty years. But the new relationship established between the two countries was so much less inequitable than any previous Anglo-Egyptian relationship that the treaty was received in Cairo with rejoicing. Before long, however, the British attempted to reoccupy western Egypt on the pretext that another war was imminent.

When they requested permission to carry out maneuvers in the Western Desert south of Fayum, I recommended that such permission be refused on the ground that it would constitute a violation of the treaty. The then Chief of Operations, Brigadier Ahmed Hamdi Himmat, agreed with me and refused to allow the maneuvers. I was not insensible to the growing danger of war, but neither was I insensible to the desire of the British to reoccupy Egypt at their first opportunity. Now that their forces had at last been confined to the Canal Zone, I was not eager to see them emerge from their confinement except in the event of an "imminent menace of war."

I also put a stop to the British habit of communicating with us through their military mission. I insisted that all communications be addressed to the Egyptian Army directly. I put a stop, too, to the custom of issuing Egyptian military orders in both English and Arabic. I had no objection to providing the British with Arabic copies of our orders, but I insisted that it was no part of our obligations under the treaty to provide them with a free translation service.

In 1937, in addition to my other duties, I founded *The Magazine of the Egyptian Army,* which I edited for several years and to which I contributed many articles. One of my favorite themes was the need for providing Egyptian high school and college students with military training. It is still my belief that military training for both sexes is essential to good citizenship in a rapidly developing but still backward, impoverished, and largely illiterate country. The Young Men's Moslem, Christian, and Hebrew Associations, their feminine auxiliaries, the Boy Scouts, the Girl Guides, the Daughters of the Nile, and other private organizations have all done excellent work, but for obvious reasons they have been able to influence only a small percentage of the young people of Egypt. The Army is the only institution capable of reaching the younger generation as a whole, without distinction as to race, class, creed, or sex, and of inculcating the pride, discipline, and spirit of self-sacrifice necessary to overcome our tremendous social, economic, and political problems within a reasonable length of time. The purpose of the military, as I have said, is to defend a government from its enemies, foreign and domestic. One of the best ways of doing so, as Turkey, Mexico, and certain other renascent countries have demonstrated, is to so strengthen a country's social, economic, and political fabric—with the help of enlightened military training—that its enemies, foreign or domestic, will not be tempted to resort to armed intervention.

In 1938 the British requested permission to send two battalions to Mersa Matruh in order to "acquaint them with the terrain." Out of curiosity, I asked them which two battalions they intended to send. When they replied that they intended to send the same two battalions from the 1st Essex Regiment and the 5th Northumberland Fusiliers that had been stationed at Mersa Matruh in 1935, I advised Abd el Wahab, the Adjutant General, to refuse their request on the ground that these two battalions were already as well acquainted with the terrain as they had any legitimate need to be. I was afraid that the British were merely seeking once again to establish a precedent for violating the Treaty of 1936, according to which no members of the British Armed Forces other than small parties of officers in civilian dress on topographical and planning missions were to be stationed west of the Nile in the absence of "war or an imminent menace of war." Abd el Wahab sent me to Lieutenant General Ali Fahmi, the Minister of War, who was just about to countersign a letter of approval. After hearing my arguments, he destroyed the letter and dictated a new one, politely but firmly refusing the British request.

Not long afterward I was named to accompany an Egyptian military mission to England, but at the last minute I was refused a visa. My name, it developed, had been placed on the blacklist of the British military mission in Cairo. Later, when I applied for admittance to the Staff Officers' School, which was still run by the British, my application was rejected. I was finally admitted in the autumn of 1938, however, at the personal insistence of Hassan Sabri, the civilian who had succeeded Ali Fahmi as the Minister of War, and in 1939 I was permitted to visit England with the other members of my class.

IX

My first son was born on March 5, 1938. I wanted to name him Saláh ed Din, in honor of the great Sultan (better known in the West as "Saladin"), but my wife, in the belief that it would bring him luck, wanted to name him Faruk. We argued the point good-naturedly for several days, but toward the end I lost my patience.

"If we must name him for a king," I said, "let's name him George. The King of England has always been luckier than the King of Egypt."

My wife, as I later learned, had already won the argument, for the midwife, without consulting me, had registered his name as

Faruk. Someday, if I can ever find the time to do so, I intend to have his name officially changed to Saláh ed Din, although it will probably be an empty gesture. The name Faruk has stuck in spite of my objections, and so, too, I am sorry to say, has the name George, which is Faruk's family nickname. Even I sometimes forget to call him Saláh ed Din.

In the summer of 1938, a few months after my son was born, I first met King Faruk. I had just been promoted to the rank of major and was temporarily in charge of the Military Museum in Cairo in the absence of its director, who had been assigned to visit similar museums in Europe. Faruk, whose acquisitive instincts were even stronger than his father's, had decided to start a private arms collection of his own. I was ordered to drive down to Alexandria, where he was spending the summer, to present him with two truckloads of exhibits. Faruk was eighteen at the time and I was thirty-seven. It was a very hot day, and the King was taking a bath when my men and I arrived at Montazah Palace in two pickup trucks. We were told to unload our trucks and await His Majesty in the palace garden. Although we were in full uniform, in spite of the heat, Faruk chose to appear before us naked from the waist up, wearing nothing but a sun helmet, slacks, and sandals without socks.

Among the contents of the trucks were two small guns. One was a brass cannon dating from the reign of Ismail, Faruk's grandfather; the other was a whale gun of about the same period. My soldiers were so nervous in the King's presence that I held the guns in my own hands for fear that they might drop them.

"Oh, Major," said Faruk. "You're so strong! What do you eat, beans?"

He then held the guns in his own hands to show that he was just as strong as I was. As he did so, I was struck by the flabbiness of his muscles and the rolls of fat on his chest. I was twice his age, but my body was in far better condition.

I stayed with Faruk in Montazah Palace for six days. He was interested in what I had to tell him about the weapons on display at the museum, but not so interested that it would ever occur to him to visit the museum himself. One night I showed him some lantern slides, which he borrowed and never returned to the museum. He was eager to know where he could find the oldest Egyptian gun. I told him that Ismail had bought a lot of Krupp's original cannons, dating from 1871, four of which were standing in the garden of the District Administration Building at Giza. Faruk ordered me to bring him one of the earliest guns and one of the earliest shells manufactured in Egypt during the reign of his great-great-grandfather, Mohammed Ali. Much against my will, I drove to Giza in the pickup and requisitioned two of the Krupp guns in the name of the King. I also requisitioned one each of Mohammed Ali's guns and shells from a collection on display at the Polytechnical School in Cairo.

Faruk, on receiving the loot, was as happy as a little boy with a new collection of toys. When the time came to remove the detonator from the shell, which was still alive, Captain Abd el Ghaffar Osman, who was later to become the King's ordnance adviser, was on hand to lend me his assistance. He kneeled to kiss Faruk's hand when he came up to watch the proceedings, even though I had ordered him to salute the King, as I did, in a manner becoming an officer.

It was on this occasion that I first met Antonio Pulli, the Italian electrician who had become the King's confidential adviser. Pulli, who had been swimming with Faruk in the palace pool, had sense enough to dress before he appeared before me and my soldiers in the garden. Faruk, however, appeared as usual dressed in nothing but slacks and sandals.

We then proceeded to disarm the shell. Osman was so eager to display his military knowledge before the King that he pushed me aside and began to unscrew the core himself. Instead of unscrewing it in a clockwise direction, he tried in vain to unscrew it in a counterclockwise direction, forgetting that shell cores are always threaded in reverse in order to prevent their being loosened by the clockwise torque of the shell in flight. I tried to indicate what was wrong, but the King, who had understood, winked at me and put his fingers to his lips. He then pushed Osman aside and began to unscrew the core in the proper clockwise direction.

"Who trained you to be a soldier?" he said.

When Osman told him that he had received his military training in England, even as the King himself, Faruk replied that he would have done better to attend the Egyptian Military Academy.

Osman, I should add, was eventually promoted to the rank of lieutenant colonel and decorated with the Order of the Nile. It was he who purchased the defective Italian hand grenades that blew up in the faces of our soldiers in Palestine. The Tribunal of the Revolution has since stripped him of his rank and his illegal fortune and sentenced him to fifteen years in prison.

During my first term at the Staff Officers' School, to which I was finally admitted in the autumn of 1938, I found it so difficult to get along with my British instructors that I lost interest in my work. During my second term, however, I recovered my equanimity and managed to graduate with the highest marks in my class. The King came to the school on graduation day to present us with our diplomas. Brigadier Zaki Kemál, the commandant, warned us before Faruk's arrival that we would be expected to kiss his hand. I told my classmates that I would not kiss anybody's hand in any circumstances and urged them to follow my example. None of them did. As for myself, I disguised my refusal by pretending to be confused. After saluting the King, I shook his hand instead of kissing it. I shook it so hard, in fact, that he winced, as was revealed in a picture that appeared that evening in one of the newspapers.

x

In the summer of 1939 my classmates and I visited France and England on a two months' tour of study. In France we inspected the Maginot Line and the battlefields of the First World War; in England we inspected a number of armaments works, military schools, and tank factories. It was my first and, so far, my last trip to Europe, and it made a deep impression on me. It made me ashamed, for one thing, of the irresponsible beys and pashas who used to visit Europe on pleasure trips but who never thought of improving the living conditions of their own people. It made me realize, too, how differently the British behaved in England from the way they behaved in Egypt. In Egypt they had become so calloused in their dealings with the "natives" that they often forgot that Egyptians had feelings too. In England, however, they were so considerate that I found it hard to believe that they were the same people. If they had only been as considerate toward Egyptians in Egypt, they would have aroused far less antipathy; but then, too, they would have realized the folly of attempting, in the twentieth century, to maintain a nineteenth-century imperial relationship with a people who have always resented their unsolicited tutelage.

Our French and British hosts did their best to win us over to the Allied cause. To some extent they did. No one who visits France and England can fail to admire the great achievements of their respective civilizations. But our hosts failed in their efforts to convince us that they would win the war. The sickly mood of the French was not that of a people who were likely to be victorious. The mood of the British was healthier, but their military preparations were so inadequate that I did not see how the Germans and the Italians could possibly fail to win. As an Egyptian, I was less concerned about the prospect of an Axis victory than I might have been if the British had been willing to treat my country as an ally rather than a colony. I had no desire to exchange British for German or Italian masters. At the same time I had no desire to assist the British in perpetuating their dominion. What I hoped was what I think most Arabs hoped— namely, that the war would so weaken the British and the French as to compel them to recognize the independence of every Arab state.

The war began almost as soon as I returned to Egypt, but it was some time before I was assigned to active duty. Colonel Bell, the British commandant of the Staff Officers' School, had described me in a report to Himmat, the Chief of Operations, as "an absolute tiger for work." He had gone on to predict that "if Major Naguib carries on in the Army as he did in the Staff Officers' School, he will attain a very high level."

Himmat, who had never liked me, liked me even less after receiving this report.

"As long as you're such a tiger for work," he said, "I've decided to assign you to the training section."

My job, it developed, was to supervise the belated translation of English manuals and textbooks into Arabic. Although I cannot say that I enjoyed such confining work, neither can I say that I have ever regretted the fact that I was forced to undertake it. I read and reread a large number of specialized volumes that I would otherwise have skipped. Each of them contained valuable knowledge that was to be of benefit to me in later years.

Early in 1940, as the British were preparing to engage in a series of full-dress maneuvers in the Western Desert, I succeeded in obtaining a temporary assignment to serve first with the 22nd and then with the 29th British Infantry brigades. With the 22nd I acted as assistant brigade major; later, when the brigade major of the 29th fell ill, I temporarily took his place. The first of our maneuvers failed for lack of preparation, but the second succeeded, partly because of a nine-hour reconnaissance that I had carried out beforehand. Lieutenant General O'Connor, who was later to be taken prisoner in Libya, congratulated Brigadier Leslie, my commanding officer, for the success of his maneuver. Leslie was good enough to give me most of the credit for his success. O'Connor asked me if there was anything he could do to express his gratitude. I told him that I would like to continue serving with the British for three more months in order to gain experience. O'Connor did his best to retain my services, but within a few weeks I was recalled to Cairo.

XI

On June 24, 1940, fifteen minutes after I had been promoted to the rank of lieutenant colonel, my second son was born. My wife and I agreed at once to call him Ali, in honor of my brother.

Italy had meanwhile entered the war and was again massing troops in Libya. This time there could be no doubt as to the Italians' intentions of invading Egypt. In co-operation with the

British, therefore, we began to fortify the whole country in the expectation of imminent hostilities. I was one of two staff officers assigned to prepare the defense of Cairo. My orders were to deliver, within forty-eight hours, detailed plans for the fortification of twenty-three strategic sites, including the water works, the electric light plant, the telephone building, and several bridges. By going without sleep and paying two clerks to do my typing for me, I was able to deliver my plans on time—and, to my surprise, they were accepted.

The long-awaited Italian invasion, which began on September 13, was halted at Sidi Barrani four days later. Instead of pushing on to Mersa Matruh and El Alamein, as they could have done, and were in fact expected to do, the Italians chose to wait for the outnumbered British to mount a counteroffensive. This began on December 10, and it was so successful that within two months fewer than 25,000 British troops had occupied all of Cyrenaica and killed or captured more than half of the Italians' army of 200,000 men.

Thus ended the Italian threat to Egypt. The German threat, which was far more serious, persisted until November 4, 1942, when it, too, ended in a British victory—the memorable Battle of El Alamein. In all this time, however, I was unable to do anything more for my country than to stand and wait. It was a posture that may have served in some small way, but it was intensely painful to an officer as eager as I was to see active duty.

Nor were the German and Italian threats the only threats that Egypt faced. As always, there was the British threat, which increased in proportion as the strategic importance of Egypt increased in the defense of the British Empire. During the war we suffered countless humiliations at the hands of the British, who failed, and still fail, to understand that our national interests are not, and can never be, the same as theirs. Of no country did the British demand more than they did of Egypt during the war, and of no country's interests were they less considerate. They expected Egyptians to behave as loyal allies while being treated as conquered subjects. Their troops marched through the streets of Cairo singing obscene songs about our King, a man whom few of us admired, but who, nevertheless, was as much of a national symbol as our flag. Faruk was never so popular as when he was being insulted in public by British troops, for we knew, as they knew, that by insulting our unfortunate King they were insulting the Egyptian people as a whole. They molested our women, assaulted our men, and committed acts of vandalism in public places. I was involved in several incidents myself. Once, when a drunken British soldier persisted in insulting the passengers in a bus in which I was traveling, I had to remove him from the vehicle by force. Again, when I was traveling in civilian clothes on a rapid-transit car between Cairo and Heliopolis, I was assaulted by three drunken South African soldiers, one of whom hit me over the head with a beer bottle and stole my wallet.

It gives me no pleasure to recall such episodes, which I would like to forget, and I mention them only to explain why so many Egyptians were less than enthusiastic in supporting the British cause. I realize, of course, that soldiers of every nationality behave badly in time of war, and that the British, if anything, behave less badly than most. But it was too much to expect ordinary Egyptians to view their treatment philosophically. All they knew was that Egypt was occupied by the British Army, as always, and that its soldiers treated them like dirt.

Is it any wonder that they often cheered Britain's enemies? In so doing, they were not supporting Fascism any more than they were opposing "democracy." Like the Irish, they were simply applauding the powers that promised to rid them of a hated occupation.

On February 1, 1942, a few days after Benghazi had been retaken by the Germans, student groups in Cairo demonstrated in favor of Ali Maher, a leading anti-British politician. The next day King Faruk dismissed the pro-British government headed by Hussein Sirri. He did so not only because of the demonstrations but also because Sirri, without bothering to consult him, had broken diplomatic relations with Vichy France at the request of the British Embassy. On February 3, before Faruk had time to consult with Maher regarding the formation of a new government, Sir Miles Lampson, the British ambassador, called at Abdín Palace. Lampson informed the King that, in view of the military situation, he would have to insist on the formation of a government headed by Mustafa en Nahass, whom the British then trusted as much as they distrusted Maher. Faruk told Lampson that he would consult a number of politicians, including Nahass as well as Maher, before coming to a decision. On February 4, before he could announce his decision, Lampson saw fit to warn him that "unless I hear by 6 P.M. that Nahass Pasha has been asked to form a cabinet, His Majesty King Faruk must expect the consequences."

At six the chief of the royal cabinet, Ahmed Hassanein, called at the British Embassy to inform Lampson that the King, after consulting numerous politicians, had decided to reject his ultimatum. Lampson told Hassanein that he would visit the King at nine. At that hour a column of British tanks, accompanied by several hundred motorized troops, forced the gates of Abdín Palace without encountering any serious resistance from the Royal

Guards. The ambassador, accompanied by General Stone, the then commander of British Troops in Egypt, and two other officers, marched upstairs to the King's chambers. After informing Faruk that he was a prisoner of the British Army, Lampson gave him his choice of signing either of two documents, which he handed him. One proclaimed Faruk's abdication, the other the appointment of Nahass. Reports differ as to whether the documents were written in English or in Arabic. They also differ as to what Faruk said to Lampson after he had chosen to sign Nahass's appointment as Prime Minister. The facts are that he signed it and that the British, as he is said to have predicted, have regretted Lampson's behavior ever since.[1]

The next day, before taking office, Nahass notified Lampson that he was forming a cabinet on the understanding that neither the Treaty of 1936 nor Egypt's position as a sovereign, independent country "permits the Ally to intervene in internal affairs and particularly in the formation and dismissal of cabinets."

The facts remain that the King of Egypt allowed the British ambassador to usurp his powers and that the Prime Minister of Egypt allowed himself to be appointed to office by the same British ambassador. I was so disgusted that I sent Faruk the following note:

"Since the Army was given no opportunity to defend Your Majesty, I am ashamed to wear my uniform. I hereby request permission to resign from the Egyptian Army."

---

[1]Its only modern parallel, so far as I am aware, is Andrei Vyshinsky's behavior toward King Michael of Romania in 1945. When Michael hesitated to appoint the Russian candidate for Prime Minister, Petru Groza, Vyshinsky warned him in person that his failure to do so would be regarded as a "hostile act" that would make it impossible for Russia "to guarantee the further independence of Romania." The fact that Romania lost its independence anyhow, as did all of Russia's victims, is no excuse for Great Britain's refusal to recognize Egypt's independence.

Faruk's reply was to send his Sudanese military aide, Brigadier (later Major General) Abdullah el Nagumi, to see me. Nagumi explained that, since the King himself had forbidden the Royal Guards to resist the British, he could not permit me to resign.

My third and last son was born on January 3, 1943. We named him Yussef in honor of my father. In 1944, I was promoted to the rank of colonel and appointed deputy governor of Sinai. Nine months later I became the governor of the Eastern Desert. In order to be promoted, however, it was necessary for me to take active command of a battalion, and so I was later transferred back to the regular Army. Thus it was that in 1947 I was placed in command of the 2nd Machine Gun Battalion at El Arísh.

In the meantime the British had again evacuated all of Egypt except the Canal Zone, and the British Government, in opening negotiations to revise the Treaty of 1936, had expressed its willingness to evacuate even the Canal Zone by September 1, 1949. The Egyptian Government had agreed in return to the creation of a Joint Defense Board to advise both governments as to the common action to be taken in the event of war arising from an attack on Egypt or any adjacent country. The agreement, signed by Ismail Sidki, the Egyptian Prime Minister, and Ernest Bevin, the British Foreign Secretary, however, was doomed to die at birth. The British Government, while agreeing to pursue a joint policy "within the framework of the unity between . . . Sudan and Egypt under the common crown of Egypt," refused to admit any limitation on its power to govern Sudan in accordance with the inequitable Agreement of 1899. Sidki, who had staked his future on his ability to come to terms with the British on both the Suez and the Sudan issues, was forced to resign. His successor, Mahmúd Fahmi el Nokrashi, appealed to the Security Council of the United Nations, but to no avail. The British remained in the

Canal Zone and continued to rule Sudan in defiance of Egypt's natural right to a voice in determining that country's political future. The demoralization that followed the collapse of the Sidki-Bevin Agreement did much to promote the graft and corruption that contributed so heavily to Egypt's defeat in Palestine.

3

THE COUP D'ETAT

By the time I became its director general, in August 1949, even the Frontier Corps had been corrupted. Brigadier Hussein Sirri Amer,[1] its chief of staff, had been named repeatedly in connection with the drug traffic and the illicit sale of state lands. He had also been accused of buying munitions left behind by the various armies that had fought in the Western Desert and of reselling them to the Egyptian Army at exorbitant prices. He was removed from the Frontier Corps in the hope of concealing the fact, which was not generally known at the time, that he and his henchmen had been sharing their profits with the King.

Even I was unaware of the fact that the King himself was involved in the arms racket until the spring of 1950. In the meantime I had foolishly kept Faruk informed of my efforts to put a stop to the racket by seizing all the arms I could find and arresting

[1]No relation to either Hussein Sirri, the politician, or Abd el Hakím Amer, of the Free Officers.

everyone who attempted to hide or sell them. The Wafd had won
the elections that year and the Prime Minister was again Nahass.
I appealed to Nahass, through Mohammed Fuad Serag ed Din,
his Minister of Interior, who was also to become his Minister of
Finance, to initiate the reforms that were necessary to save Egypt
from disaster. It was my hope, which Abd el Nasser and the other
members of the executive committee shared, that it might not be
necessary for the Free Officers to revolt at all if the proper reforms
were carried out in time. We exhausted every possibility of chang-
ing conditions peacefully before we resorted to the use of force. We
circulated numerous clandestine leaflets in which we called attention to the more flagrant abuses that we were determined to correct. We also distributed reprints of a nine-page report that I had
written, and of which I had delivered typewritten copies to
Nahass, Serag ed Din, and Mustafa Nusrat, the then Minister of
War. We wheedled, cajoled, and threatened, but the King and
his cronies on the one hand, and Nahass and his cronies on the
other, refused to take us seriously. They referred to us as "children" and warned us, without knowing who we were, to leave
politics to the initiated and confine ourselves to military matters.

We succeeded, however, in forcing Nahass to authorize an investigation of the Ministry of War. The investigation resulted in
the indictment of thirteen persons, including Prince Abbas Halím,
a cousin of the King. Prince Abbas was accused, among other
things, of misappropriating $400,000 of the secret funds advanced
in dollars to cover his expenses in obtaining arms for Egypt in
defiance of the UN's embargo. Mohammed Azmi, the Prosecutor
General, went on to examine the bank accounts and safe-deposit
boxes of other suspects and their wives. Antonio Pulli, the King's
confidential adviser, was alerted in time to clean out his safe-
deposit boxes before they could be examined. But Edmond

Gahlan, the King's straw man in the arms racket, was not so lucky. He had been summering with the King in France and was unable to reach Cairo in time to prevent Azmi and his investigators from examining his checkbooks. They were thus able to draw up a list of all the persons, including Faruk himself, to whom Gahlan had been making payments from his special account with the Cairo branch of the Banque Belge et Internationale. The list was a veritable Who's Who in Egyptian Graft and Corruption. Gahlan, who had been posing as an importer of American fountain pens, had collected more than a million pounds in bribes from the various arms dealers who had been supplying Egypt with antiquated and defective weapons.

The Prosecutor General was promptly ordered to quash his investigation on pain of being imprisoned for lese majesty—the crime of "injuring the dignity" of the King. Azmi did as he was told. He even allowed Gahlan to escape from custody in order to rejoin the King in France. But by then it was common knowledge that the King and his cronies had made a fortune out of the Palestine disaster.

The arms scandal was succeeded, in the autumn of 1950, by a cotton scandal involving Zeinab el Wakil en Nahass, the aging Prime Minister's grasping and still youthful wife. Madame Nahass was accused of rigging the Alexandria cotton exchange with the help of Serag ed Din and several other members of her husband's cabinet.

In September 1950, I made my first pilgrimage to Mecca. My daughter Samiha had been stricken with leukemia and I was badly in need of religious inspiration. Samiha, who was then nineteen, had been studying law at Cairo University. There was nothing that I or anyone could do to save her life. All I could do was to pray in the mosque at Mecca for the strength to bear my sorrow and the wisdom to do God's bidding in my effort to change the course of Egypt's destiny. Samiha died a few weeks after I returned to Cairo. I was still in mourning when I was informed in December that I had at last been promoted to the rank of major general.

Partly for reasons of patriotism, and partly to hide the corruption of its leaders, the Wafd, in association with various extremist groups, embarked on a bloody but ineffectual "war of liberation" against the British forces in the Canal Zone. The guerrilla war for the most part was waged by armed civilians, assisted from time to time by the auxiliary police force called the *Buluk el Nizám*. Several members of the Free Officers assisted in training the "liberation units," as they were called, but as an organization we remained aloof. Although we sympathized with their objectives, we distrusted the motives of the men who had called them into being.

During 1951 some 40,000 Egyptian employees of the British were forced to give up their jobs in the Canal Zone in return for the Wafd's promise to employ them elsewhere. Inasmuch as there were no jobs available in private industry, they were added to an already overcrowded civil service. Thousands of unemployed Wafdists who had been clamoring for political rewards were added to the civil service at the same time.

In October, in an ill-timed effort to divert the Wafd from its struggle against the British, the United States invited Egypt to become a "co-equal partner" with Great Britain, France, and Turkey in its projected Middle East Defense Organization. The Wafd replied to the American maneuver by abrogating the Treaty of 1936 and the Agreement of 1899 and proclaiming Faruk the King of Sudan as well as Egypt. The fighting in the Canal Zone was resumed to the accompaniment of ominous disorders in Cairo.

It was then that King Faruk decided to reorganize the Egyptian Army. Lieutenant General Hussein Faríd became the new Chief of Staff. Sirri Amer was promoted to the rank of major general and named to succeed me as the director general of the Frontier Corps. Once again I offered to resign from the Army and once again my offer was refused. General Haidar, who was still the Commander in Chief, appointed me director general of infantry. I refused to accept the appointment at first, on the ground that it was tantamount to a demotion without cause. The director general of the Frontier Corps, which was an autonomous force, took precedence over the director general of infantry.

Abd el Nasser and Amer begged me to reconsider. If I resigned, they said, the Free Officers would be left without a single general to represent them. I was in bed with tonsillitis at the time and in no condition to argue. It was finally agreed that I should hold out for a higher post, but that, if I could not obtain one, I should accept the post of director general of infantry.

When Haidar telephoned a few days later to ask if I had changed my mind, I told him that I could not accept an appointment that would make me inferior to Sirri Amer, a man whom I thought should be in jail. Haidar attempted to convince me that the director general of infantry, who commanded a force of 30,000 men, was really more important than the director general of the Frontier Corps, who commanded a force of little more than 3000 men. When he found that he could not convince me with such arguments, he asked me to name a post that I would be willing to accept. Thinking of what it would mean to the Free Officers, I suggested that he make me director general of intelligence. But Haidar only laughed.

"You know as well as I do," he said, "that the King would never allow anyone but a close personal friend to hold such a post, and he considers you his enemy."

I wondered what Haidar meant.

"Then why not make me Adjutant General?" I said at last.

Again Haidar laughed. "Perhaps later on," he said, "but not right away. The King doesn't trust you."

He finally asked me to accept the post of director general of infantry on a trial basis. Within two months, he promised, he would either get rid of Sirri Amer, in which event he would reinstate me as director general of the Frontier Corps, or he would appoint me to a more important post. I accepted his offer for the reason I have mentioned, but I knew from experience that Haidar's promises could not be taken seriously. As events developed, his promise on this occasion was even less serious than I imagined.

II

I was worried by what Haidar had said about the King. Did it mean that Faruk was aware of my connection with the Free Officers? Or did it mean only that he resented my behavior as director general of the Frontier Corps?

At Ras el Hekma, on the Mediterranean coast between Alexandria and Mersa Matruh, the King had built himself a summer palace with stolen materials on stolen land with the use of stolen labor. The land, which he had illegally expropriated, had been reclaimed by the government at public expense. The materials belonged to the Ministry of Public Works. The labor consisted of skilled workers detached from legitimate public projects and unskilled workers detached from the Frontier Corps.

Soon after becoming its director general, I had put a stop to the practice of using soldiers detached from the Frontier Corps as guards and servants in the palace. I had also prevailed on the Minister of War to issue a decree forbidding the further sale or transfer of state lands in frontier areas pending the creation of a land board to supervise their disposition. It was for these reasons, as I was later relieved to learn, that Faruk considered me an enemy. It was for these reasons, too, that he decided to appoint Sirri Amer to succeed me as the director general of the Frontier Corps. Sirri Amer was a man of Faruk's own kidney; he boggled at nothing that redounded to his profit. I, on the other hand, was described by the King at the time as a "Don Quixote" who was "riding for a fall."

Until the election held by the Officers' Club on January 6, 1952, the executive committee of the Free Officers had assumed that it would be impossible for us to revolt before the year 1955. The election changed our minds. It was the first honest election that the club had ever held. Its officials, elective in theory, had in practice been appointed by the King. The Free Officers, after gaining control of the electoral committee, decided to use the election as a test of strength. Instead of allowing the King's candidates to be elected by default, we amended the bylaws in such a way as to require at least two candidates for every office. What prompted us to do so was the knowledge that the King was now thinking of appointing Sirri Amer to succeed Haidar.

Haidar, whose nickname was "The Jailer," was a former prison director whom the King had exceptionally promoted to the rank of lieutenant general in order to make him Commander in Chief. The highest rank he had held in the regular Army was that of a second lieutenant. Sycophant though he was, however, he was preferable to Sirri Amer, a man who was hated by every self-respecting officer.

Seventy years earlier the Egyptian Army had revolted under

Ahmed Orabi when Faruk's uncle, Khedive Tawfik, had attempted to discriminate in favor of Turkish and Albanian officers
by retiring a group of Egyptian officers on half pay. Now the
Armed Forces were asked to submit to the indignity of being commanded by a criminal.

I agreed to run for president of the Officers' Club as the candidate of the Free Officers, who were identified only as "the officers
who opposed corruption." I wanted to discover, among other
things, whether I still commanded the respect of my fellow officers
after accepting the humiliation of being replaced by Sirri Amer as
the director general of the Frontier Corps. If I lost the election, I
knew, I would be finished both as an officer and as a champion of
those who wanted an Egyptian renaissance. Faruk, in fact, warned
me indirectly that unless I withdrew my candidacy I would be
relieved even as the director general of infantry.

The results of the election surprised everyone. All of the King's
candidates were defeated and all of the Free Officers' candidates
were elected. Of the 334 votes that were cast for president, only 58
were cast for my three opponents; the remaining 276 were cast
for me. Other members of the Free Officers who were elected to
the board of governors included Squadron Leader Hassan Ibrahim
el Sayed and Lieutenant Colonel Zakaria Mohi ed Din. Mohammed Rashad Mehanna was also elected to the board of governors
although he was not a member of the Free Officers.

The King in a fury declared the election null and void. When
a majority of the club's members voted to abide by its results, he
appointed a committee to revise the bylaws once again. When we
refused to recognize the committee, he withdrew the funds he had
appropriated to complete our new clubhouse on the Sharia Fuad
in the residential district of Zamalek. We were thus compelled to
take up a collection in order to complete the building.

Faruk was so angry with Mehanna that the latter, to avoid trouble, asked to be transferred to El Arísh. Faruk was still debating whether to remove me as the director general of infantry when Egypt's destiny was abruptly changed by the cataclysm that occurred on January 26, 1952.

III

Two days earlier, in response to an ultimatum, 160 members of the *Buluk el Nizám,* the auxiliary police, had surrendered to the British at Fayid, the administrative capital of the Canal Zone. Serag ed Din, the Minister of Interior, announced in the course of a radio speech in Cairo that henceforth all policemen, regular or auxiliary, would be expected to "fight to the last bullet." Those who failed to do so, he said, would be tried before a military tribunal.

At dawn the next day 1500 British soldiers, supported by tanks and armored cars, surrounded the Governorate in Ismailía. Two hundred and fifty Egyptian policemen, regular and auxiliary, were trapped inside. Captain Mustafa Ibrahim Rifa'at, their commander, was given exactly fifteen minutes to surrender or take the consequences. Inasmuch as the British had failed to clip his wires, Rifa'at was able to telephone to Serag ed Din in Cairo to ask him what to do. Whereas he and his men were equipped only with outmoded rifles and hand grenades, he explained, the British were equipped with the latest automatic weapons as well as the cannons, large and small, of their tanks and armored cars. Serag ed Din told Rifa'at that he would be expected to carry out his orders—namely, to "fight to the last bullet."

Rifa'at did so. Nine hours later, when the last of his bullets

had been expended, he surrendered. His casualties numbered
118—forty-six dead and seventy-two wounded. Brigadier Exham,
the British commander, expressed his "admiration and respect"
for the bravery that Rifa'at and his men had displayed. The fact
remained, however, that forty-six Egyptians had been massacred
in cold blood.

On the morning of January 26, as if by prearrangement, mobs
began to gather all over Cairo. Resolute action on the part of the
government or the palace would probably have prevented the
holocaust that followed. No action of any sort was taken. Before
long the mobs were attacking and setting fire to numerous foreign
and luxury establishments. Before the Army was permitted to
re-establish order, seventeen foreigners (including nine Britons
and one Canadian) and fifty-odd Egyptians had been killed. A
British club, a Jewish school, an office of the Moslem Brotherhood, four hotels, four night clubs, seven department stores, seventeen cafés and restaurants, eighteen cinemas, and seventy other
commercial establishments, including banks, automobile display
rooms, and airline ticket offices, had been destroyed.

The rioting was still going on when my brother Ali and I arrived at Abdín Palace at one that afternoon to attend the banquet
given by Faruk in honor of the son whom his new Queen, the
former Narriman Sadek, had borne him ten days earlier. It was
not until later that we realized that Cairo was in flames. Faruk
and Haidar had seemed preoccupied throughout the banquet, but
neither had even so much as mentioned the riots. Their frequent
whispered conferences with various couriers, however, indicated
that they were aware of what was happening.

Martial law was declared at 4 P.M. Within two hours the Army
had quenched the last of the flames and dispersed the last of the
rioters. We could have restored order just as easily at any time

after 9 A.M., when the riots had begun. Why, then, were we not allowed to do so until four in the afternoon?

There are those who believe that the burning of Cairo, like the burning of Bogotá, the capital of Colombia, was a Russian plot. There are others who believe it was a British plot, others who believe it was a Wafdist plot, and still others who believe it was a palace plot. There can be no doubt that extremists in the pay of more than one Communist embassy incited the mobs to arson and murder. Why, then, was the Army not permitted to restore order at once? Serag ed Din was accused of deceiving the King by assuring him that the police were in control of the situation. Faruk, however, had his own intelligence service. Why should he have taken the word of his Minister of Interior, whom he hated, against the word of his own agents, who certainly knew what was happening? And why, after Nahass had been dismissed and Serag ed Din had been arrested, was so little evidence produced to support the government's charge that Cairo was burned at the instigation of Serag ed Din and other Wafdists acting in collaboration with foreign agents? Ahmed Hussein, the leader of the so-called Socialist Party, was also arrested. Yet, though he and several of his henchmen were tried for subversion, they were eventually acquitted for lack of sufficient evidence against them.

What really happened, I believe, is that the King and his cronies, in collaboration with British agents, attempted to create a situation that would so embarrass the Wafd as to justify the dismissal of Nahass and his cabinet, the suspension of Parliament, and the appointment of a caretaker cabinet that would obey the wishes of the King. Serag ed Din fell into the trap by allowing the rioters to be led by the only forces that were capable of burning Cairo—the Communists and their extremist dupes in half a dozen different parties. Both the King and Serag ed Din were so eager to blame each other for touching off an explosion of such appalling magnitude that each hesitated until too late to save himself from the consequences of his folly. Black Saturday, as it was called, was the end of Serag ed Din and the party that he and Madame Nahass had led to ruin. It was also the end of King Faruk.

IV

Ali Maher was appointed to succeed Nahass, but, since he hesitated to suspend the Wafdist Chamber of Deputies in order to prosecute its leaders, he was dismissed before he had been a month in office. His successor as Prime Minister was Ahmed Naguib el Hilali, a former Minister of Education who had been expelled from the Wafd in 1951 because of his opposition to the corrupt practices of its leaders. Hilali suspended Parliament, re-opened the arms and cotton investigations, arrested political extremists of every hue, and began to prosecute the corrupt leaders of the Wafd. He also re-established friendly relations with the British. Had the British reciprocated, either in the Canal Zone or in Sudan, and had the King and his cronies supported Hilali's purification program, we might never have revolted. The British, however, betrayed Hilali's hopes by drafting a constitution for Sudan that showed even less regard for Egypt's rights than the inequitable Agreement of 1899. As for the King, though he permitted Hilali to prosecute a few of the grafters associated with the Wafd, he refused to let him prosecute any of the grafters associated with the palace. Hilali's one-sided reforms were thus doomed to failure.

General Sirri Amer in the meantime had become involved in a plot to smuggle Diesel oil, scrap metals, and munitions into Israel. The scrap metals consisted of ruined military equipment left behind in the Western Desert. The Diesel oil and the munitions belonged to the Egyptian Army. Sirri Amer and his henchmen had sold them to a ring of Jewish smugglers whom they had illegally allowed to reside in Gaza. Sirri Amer had thus not only stolen government property, he had also traded with the enemy and thereby committed a crime that was tantamount to treason.

The Free Officers decided that the time had come to act. Saláh Salem, who was in charge of our clandestine propaganda, began to circulate leaflets demanding Sirri Amer's prosecution. When nothing happened, he circulated leaflets supporting the movement to make me the Minister of War. Our only quarrel with Ahmed Mortada el Maraghi, Hilali's Minister of War and Interior, was that he was occupying a post that Hilali had promised to me. It was Hilali's hope that, by making me Minister of War, he could mend the rift between the palace and the Officers' Club, of which I was still acting as president in open defiance of the King.

Faruk's answer to the demands of the Free Officers, whom his spies had thus far failed to identify, was to ask Hilali to make Sirri Amer his Minister of War. Hilali, to his credit, refused. But the mere knowledge of the King's request so infuriated my junior colleagues that, without consulting me, they prepared forthwith to assassinate Sirri Amer. They fired fourteen bullets into his car one night but succeeded only in wounding his chauffeur, who fortunately recovered. It was fortunate, too, that they escaped detection, for if any of them had been captured our revolt might never have occurred. As it was, they were so shaken by their experience that they agreed to eschew assassination as a political

weapon thereafter. They at last understood what they had failed
to understand before—namely that a man like Sirri Amer, evil
though he was, was not important enough to kill at the risk of
jeopardizing the movement.

v

Hilali was not what the King and his cronies wanted at all.
What they wanted was a Prime Minister who could be trusted
to put on a show of reform without disturbing the intricate system of bribery and corruption by which they had been enriching
themselves at the expense of the Egyptian people. Such a man,
they mistakenly thought, was Hussein Sirri. But before they could
prepare Sirri to take office, Hilali turned the tables on them by
resigning. His supporters accused Ahmed Abbúd, Egypt's leading
industrialist, of paying a tremendous bribe to the palace to name
Sirri as Hilali's successor. Abbúd, of course, denied the charge,
but the mere fact that the Hilali government had been suing him
for the recovery of LE 4,000,000 ($14,350,000) in back taxes
so weakened his denial that it was almost impossible for Sirri to
form a cabinet. Few reputable politicians were willing to join a
cabinet that was alleged to have been bought and paid for in
advance. And fewer still were willing to associate themselves with
Karím Tabet, who insisted on becoming Sirri's Minister of Propaganda.

Tabet, the principal organizer of the plot to unseat Hilali,
was the most hated of all the King's cronies. He was hated not
only because he was a former journalist and publisher who bought
and sold political influence; he was hated also because he was a
cynic who had made Egyptian Moslems look ridiculous by en-

couraging Faruk to declare himself a *sayed*—a descendant of the Prophet. Faruk, as everybody knew, was a descendant of Albanians and Circassians on his father's side and of Turks and Frenchmen on his mother's side. One of his maternal forebears, in fact, was Joseph Sèves, alias Suleiman Pasha, who had served as one of Napoleon's officers during the French invasion of Egypt in 1798. If there was any Arabic blood in Faruk's veins, it was so diluted that it couldn't possibly have been traced back to Mohammed, and it was a sacrilege for anyone to have tried to do so.

Among the others involved in the plot to oust Hilali was Faruk's valet, Mohammed Hassan el Suleimani, who had been delivering orders to the government ever since the burning of Cairo. Faruk, toward the end, was seldom at home to anyone except his trollops and toadies and an occasional international gambler. People like Mohammed Hassan, the valet, and Pulli, the former electrician, were allowed to rule Egypt by proxy with the help of creatures like Tabet and Gahlan and the late Elías Andraos, a former bookkeeper who had made a fortune in the rayon business during the war, and who had since become the royal economic adviser. Other members of the palace gang included Abd el Azíz, the butler; Mohammed Hilmi Hussein, a chauffeur and mechanic who was known as the "Director of the Royal Garages"; Hassan Akef, the chief pilot of the King's private air force; Dr. Yussef Rashád, the royal physician; and Mohammed Naguib Salem, the royal treasurer. Dr. Hafez Afifi, the chief of the royal cabinet, and Hassan Yussef, his assistant, had far less influence over the King than any of the members of his kitchen cabinet.

Sirri's official cabinet lasted exactly seventeen days. Its downfall was precipitated by a penciled note from Abd el Azíz, the butler, which Afifi handed to Sirri on July 10. The King, instead of communicating with his prime ministers directly, was in the habit of transmitting his desires to Afifi through Mohammed Hassan, if he happened to be in his living quarters; through Pulli, if he happened to be in his office or in a night club; and through Abd el Azíz, if he happened to be in the palace dining hall. Usually Afifi would edit what they told him and pass the sense of it (if it made any sense) along to whoever was Prime Minister at the time. On the day in question, however, Afifi chose to hand Sirri intact the note that he had just received from Abd el Azíz:

"Haidar must be removed within five days unless he dissolves the executive committee of the Officers' Club and removes the twelve officers who have been conspiring against His Majesty the King."

Sirri asked Afifi who the twelve officers were. Afifi told him that Haidar probably knew their names, but Haidar, on being summoned to the Prime Minister's office, denied any knowledge of our conspiracy. Sirri told him to take whatever precautions he considered necessary but to take no overt action until they had discussed the matter further.

Sirri, like Hilali, had intended to make me his Minister of War. Inasmuch as the King had refused to approve my appointment, Sirri had taken the post himself in the hope of preventing the King from giving it to Sirri Amer, whose appointment, he knew, would precipitate the very revolt that the King was hoping to avert.

On July 15, without consulting Sirri, Haidar officially dissolved the executive committee of the Officers' Club of which I was still the president. Sirri, fearing the worst, upbraided Haidar for disobeying his instructions. Haidar's only excuse was that he would have been dismissed if he had failed to obey the instructions of the King.

Faruk, I knew, had lost confidence in Haidar because of his previous failure to take any action against me. He was thinking of appointing Lieutenant General Hussein Faríd, the then Chief of Staff, to succeed Haidar as Commander in Chief of the Armed Forces. Faríd would banish me to Mangabad, in Upper Egypt, and appoint Sirri Amer to succeed him as Chief of Staff if the King, in the meantime, failed to persuade Sirri to make him his Minister of War.

Sirri decided to make an issue of my case. His son-in-law, Mohammed Hashem, who had succeeded Maraghi as Minister of Interior, asked me to do nothing until Sirri had made a final effort to obtain the King's consent to my becoming his Minister of War. Everyone seemed to assume by then, without actually knowing what was going on, that I was not only the president of the Officers' Club but also the leader of "the twelve officers" whom Faruk had been waiting for Haidar to remove.

Sirri, true to his promise, informed Faruk through Afifi that he would be forced to resign unless the King permitted him to appoint me Minister of War with full power to purge the Armed Forces. It was three days before he received the King's reply from Afifi, in the form of a note from Mohammed Hassan, the valet:

"Dismiss Naguib and appoint Haidar Minister of War."

Haidar, who had been worried sick by the King's apparent determination to dismiss him, now informed Sirri that Faruk had decided to forgive him on condition that he appoint Faríd Commander in Chief and Sirri Amer Chief of Staff. Tabet, it seemed, had convinced the King that his quarrel with the Officers' Club was nothing more than a "tempest in a teapot." The solution he proposed was to dismiss me from the Army and, if necessary, try me for treason.

VI

Sirri resigned on the night of July 19. That morning several members of the executive committee of the Free Officers met with me at my home in the outskirts of Cairo. Among them were Abd el Nasser, Amer, Squadron Leader (now Wing Commander) Hassan Ibrahim el Sayed, and Major Kemál ed Din Hussein. We unanimously agreed that Egypt was now fully ripe for a revolution. Almost everybody who was anybody in Egyptian politics was either abroad or in Alexandria, where the King was in summer residence at Montazah Palace. Sirri's potential successors, we knew, would be plotting one against the other in their summer homes or in such hotels as the Cecil, which was the traditional center of Alexandrian intrigue. It was so hot and sultry that no one besides ourselves would be thinking in terms of an immediate revolution. It was therefore the ideal time for us to strike. Our best chance of saving the country would be to act at once, before the King had time to appoint another cabinet, and before his spies had time to discover who we were and what we had in mind. Our first objective would be to seize power and appoint a Prime Minister who would be sympathetic to our cause. Our second objective would be to allay the fears of the British, the Americans, and other foreigners who might suspect us of acting on behalf of the Communists or the Moslem Brothers. Our third objective would be to get rid of the King as soon as we had established ourselves in power. We resolved to do everything possible to avoid bloodshed, but not to shrink from it if necessary to attain our ends.

A score of picked officers were warned to expect telephone calls at their homes at nine o'clock every night until further notice. They were all trusted members of the Free Officers whom we regarded as potential future members of the executive committee. Only the ten members of the committee, however, were informed of all our plans; the others were told only what they needed to know in order to perform the tasks assigned to them.

The other members of the original executive committee, whom I was not to meet until after the Revolution, were Wing Commander Gamál ed Din Mustafa Salem (Saláh Salem's elder brother), Wing Commander Abd el Latíf Baghdadi, Lieutenant Colonel (now Colonel) Anwar es Sadát, and Major Khaled Mohi ed Din. Four of the other officers whom I have mentioned were added to the executive committee on the eve of the coup d'état. They were Lieutenant Colonel Zakaria Mohi ed Din (an elder cousin of Khaled Mohi ed Din), Lieutenant Colonel Hussein el Shafei, Lieutenant Colonel Abd el Moneim Amín, and Lieutenant Colonel Yussef Saddík Mansúr. The executive committee would later become the Council of the Revolution. Three of its fourteen members, unfortunately, would have to be removed. The wife of one was suspected of trying to exploit her husband's influence; the other two were suspected Communists.

At the time of the coup d'état the average age of the fourteen members of the executive committee was thirty-four. I, who was then fifty-one, was five years older than the second oldest, Saddík Mansúr, who was then forty-six. Khaled Mohi ed Din, the youngest, was twenty-nine. The rest of the Free Officers, who numbered several hundred, were divided into cells of not less than three or more than five members each. No member of any cell knew more than one member of the executive fourteen. It was thus possible for us to maintain the secrecy that produced the surprise that guaranteed the success of the coup d'état.

VII

Abd el Nasser's original plan was to strike at one o'clock on
the morning of August 5, but I insisted on acting sooner in the
conviction that we would not be able to maintain secrecy for
more than a very few days. On the night of July 20 the King
astonished his cronies by reappointing Hilali, and Hilali astonished everybody by making Ismail Sherín his Minister of War.
The news was so disturbing that, for fear of being discovered,
we advanced the date of the coup to July 22. In the end, though,
we found it impossible to make all the necessary arrangements
in time to act before the morning of Wednesday, July 23.

By then Hilali had taken office and Sherín had begun to consult with Haidar and other senior officers concerning the advisa-
bility of ordering my arrest. On the afternoon of July 22, I was
told by a certain journalist, whom I met at the Rowing Club,
that I was to be retired instead. That evening one of the Free
Officers, acting on his own and knowing nothing of our plans,
called at my house to confirm what the journalist had told me.
He added that I was suspected of being the leader of a group
of conspirators who were about to be arrested. I did my best to
conceal my alarm.

It was nine-thirty before the officer left my house and much
too late for me to warn my colleagues of their danger. Each of
them, if our plans had not miscarried, would already have begun
to perform his appointed task. Baghdadi would have seized control of the air base at Almaza, in the outskirts of Cairo, and he
and Ibrahim would have begun to brief their pilots for the role
that they would play at dawn. Shafei, with Khaled Mohi ed Din,

would have seized control of the cavalry, while Amín would have seized control of the artillery. Saddík and Hussein would have seized control of the infantry. The Salem brothers, with Sadát and Amer, would have flown to Sinai, Gamál to seize control of all the forces based at El Arísh, Saláh to seize control of the land forces based at Rafa. Sadát and Amer would then have rejoined Abd el Nasser in Cairo, where Zakaria Mohi ed Din and his men would be preparing to arrest all senior officers likely to oppose us.

Although I was at all times in actual command, my movements were being so closely watched that I would only have jeopardized our chances of success had I attempted to play an active role from the very beginning. It was agreed, therefore, that I should remain at home until the first phase of the revolt had been completed. Only then was I to join my junior colleagues at the Headquarters Building in Kubri el Kubba. In the meantime, if anyone in authority telephoned or came to see me, I was to calm his fears if I could, or mislead him if I could not.

H Hour was one o'clock on the morning of July 23. Given the late hours observed by most Egyptians during the hot summer months, it was the earliest that we could reasonably expect the streets to be deserted and the authorities to be in bed. Actually we were not allowed to wait that long. A certain officer who suspected our intentions betrayed us to the palace. By eleven-thirty on July 22 the Chief of Staff, General Faríd, had received orders to arrest every officer suspected of disloyalty to the King. He in turn alerted a number of his subordinates, one of whom was my brother Ali, who was then the commander of the Cairo military district.

Ali's worried wife telephoned at 1 A.M. to tell me that he had left home at midnight and had not yet returned. I promised to find out what had happened to him. He told me when I telephoned to him at GHQ that a coup was expected and that Abdín Palace was already surrounded.

"Who told you that?" I said.

"The police."

"I wouldn't take the police too seriously. They're always telling stories."

"I know, but General Faríd——"

I told him not to take Faríd too seriously either and added that the talk about a coup was nonsense. I then informed him of his wife's telephone call and advised him to go home and go to bed.

An hour later I received a long-distance call from Maraghi, the Minister of Interior, in Alexandria.

"I appeal to you as a soldier and a patriot," he said, "to put a stop to this affair."

"What do you mean?" My tone was as disingenuous as I could make it.

"You know what I mean. Your boys have started something in Kubri el Kubba, and if you don't put a stop to it the British may intervene."

"I don't know what you're talking about," I said, "and, besides, how do I know you're Maraghi? For all I know you may be only trying to find an excuse for arresting me."

Maraghi hung up after telling me that the Prime Minister would call me presently. In the meantime, he said, he hoped that I would do as he requested in the best interests of the country.

Hilali's Minister of Propaganda, Faríd Za'aluk, was the next person to call me from Alexandria. He had evidently been talking to Maraghi, for he immediately identified himself by recalling that, at my request, he had once helped some Sudanese nationalists who had been unjustly deprived of their Egyptian civil rights.

Za'aluk also appealed to me to halt the coup d'état. Unless I did, he said, the British would reoccupy Egypt and we would all be worse off than before. I told him that he was dreaming of a danger that did not exist; and, if it did exist, it was something beyond my power to control.

Our original plan was to take the Headquarters Building in Kubri el Kubba by stealth. Only after we had occupied GHQ, with its vital communications center, were our motorized and armored forces to have entered Cairo. Now, because of the betrayal I have mentioned, the building was ablaze with light and full of officers who had been alerted to put down our coup d'état. There was nothing to do but lay siege to the building and take it by force. Its occupants surrendered after putting up a token resistance in the course of which two men were killed. These, plus two others who were wounded in a skirmish in the Air Force barracks at Almaza, were the only casualties suffered in the Cairo area.

By the time GHQ was taken it was one forty-five. Tanks and armored cars and thousands of impatient soldiers in all sorts of vehicles had assembled on the Sharia Khalifa el Ma'amún, the main avenue leading into Cairo. They were now ordered to occupy the city without further delay.

VIII

At two-thirty, when I had received no word of what was happening, I said my prayers and then telephoned to GHQ. I was told that Phase One was under way but had not yet been completed. I was also told that Ali had been taken prisoner and was asked if I wanted him to be released. I said that I thought it would be better to hold Ali along with the other prisoners until we had consolidated our position. Ali was not against us, but neither was he with us. For weeks I had been avoiding him for fear of arousing his suspicion. He would probably have joined us had I asked him to, but I was opposed in principle to letting more than one member of a given family risk his life. The others, if we failed, were entitled to survive. Now that he was a prisoner, I thought, it would be best to treat Ali impartially so that, if we failed, he would not be unjustly suspected of having been privy to our plot.

Zakaria Mohi ed Din's security teams had meanwhile completed their arrests. In addition to Faríd himself, the prisoners included General Ahmed Tala'at, the chief of police; General Abd el Monsef Mahmúd, the Undersecretary of Interior; Major General Mohammed Imám, the chief of the political police; and Brigadier Hassan Hishmat, the commander of the Armored Corps. Faríd had ordered Hishmat to "find out what was going on," and the latter, in attempting to do so, had played right into our hands. He and several of his subordinates were arrested after they had driven into the main barracks at Abbassía. The others had been arrested either at GHQ or in their homes.

At three-thirty a Free Officer telephoned to say that Phase One had been completed and that he was sending some armored cars to my house to escort me to GHQ. I told him that I would prefer to use my own car, a gray Opel which I had recently purchased on the installment plan. It proved to be the last time that I would be allowed to use it. Halfway to GHQ, I was met by a column of armored cars and transferred to a jeep. My frightened chauffeur drove the Opel back to my house, where he told my wife that I had been arrested. Fortunately my wife was not unduly alarmed, and so I had only one hysterical woman—Ali's wife—to deal with in the morning. From then until the day I became Prime Minister, I was persuaded to use General Faríd's yellow Chevrolet; thereafter I was driven about in one of the Cadillac sedans belonging to the government's motor pool. My house is not equipped with a garage, and so my little Opel has been parked under a tent in the garden ever since.

Soon after reaching GHQ, I received the promised telephone call from Hilali in Alexandria. It was no longer necessary for me to feign ignorance of what was happening. I therefore told him that the Free Officers had seized power in order to assist the Egyptian Government in carrying out its avowed task of purifying the country. No one except the corruptionists had any cause for alarm. Hilali asked me what we intended to do. I told him that it was too early to say, but that I would keep him informed of our plans as they developed.

Then Maraghi telephoned to ask me to come to Alexandria to see him. I told him that if he wanted to see me he would have to come to Cairo. He suggested that I meet him at the Ministry of War at 7 A.M. I said that my bodyguard would be waiting for him at the Ministry to escort him to my headquarters. Maraghi actually flew up to Cairo, but somehow we missed connections.

A few minutes later Haidar telephoned to say that all would be forgiven if I called off the coup. The King was ready to appoint me Minister of War. I told Haidar that I would consider his proposal but that I could promise nothing.

In the meantime one of our officers had explained the general purposes of our revolt to an attaché of the American Embassy in Cairo. Ambassador Jefferson Caffery and his immediate staff were in Alexandria with the government, as were the principal officers of the other foreign diplomatic missions, including Michael

J. Creswell, the British minister, who was acting as chargé d'affaires in the absence of his ambassador, Sir Ralph Skrine Stevenson. Had Caffery been in Cairo we would have approached him directly, even though none of us had ever met him, for he was one of the few foreign diplomats whom we believed that we could trust. The only member of the Free Officers who knew anyone at the American Embassy was Squadron Leader Ali Sabri, then the chief of Air Force intelligence. He was authorized to awaken Lieutenant Colonel David L. Evans, the assistant American Air Force attaché, and inform him in general terms of what we had in mind. Sabri, in accordance with his instructions, requested Evans to inform his ambassador and to request his ambassador, in turn, to inform the British chargé d'affaires that the revolt was a purely internal matter affecting Egyptians only; that foreign lives and property would be zealously respected; and that so long as the British refrained from intervening they would be treated in the same manner as other foreigners. Sabri requested Evans to warn his ambassador, however, that if the British intervened it would be they, and not the Free Officers, who would be responsible for the bloodshed that would inevitably ensue. Sabri, of course, was careful not to mention our plan to dethrone the King.

It was fortunate, I think, that the British ambassador was at home on leave. Although Sir Ralph Stevenson was personally as reasonable as any ambassador the British have ever sent to Egypt, he might have been given unreasonable instructions had he been in Alexandria at the time. In his absence, the British Government was probably less inclined than it would otherwise have been to intervene. We were fearful, even so, lest the British forces in the Canal Zone be tempted to occupy the Delta on the pretext of saving foreign lives and property. Events would prove that our fears were not unjustified.

IX

As soon as our forces had completed the occupation of Cairo, Anwar es Sadát proceeded to the studios of the Egyptian State Broadcasting Company to read the following proclamation in my name:

"To my brothers, the sons of the Nile:

"You know that our country has been living through delicate moments, and you have seen the hands of traitors at work in its affairs. These traitors dared to extend their influence to the Army, imagining that it was devoid of patriotic elements.

"We have therefore decided to purify ourselves, to eliminate the traitors and weaklings, and thus record a new and honorable page in the history of our country.

"Those who engage in destructive activities will be severely punished. The Army will co-operate with the police in maintaining order.

"In conclusion, I would like to reassure our brothers, the foreigners who live among us, that their interests will be respected. The Army will be fully responsible for their lives and property."

I identified myself as the Commander in Chief of the Egyptian Armed Forces. A professional announcer repeated the proclamation every half hour until I was able to appear in person to address another message to the people.

Since dawn our piston bombers and jet fighters had been flying over Cairo, Alexandria, and the other cities of the Delta. Tanks and armored cars had taken up positions in front of public build-

ings and in many of the main squares of Cairo. If any resistance
had been encountered, they would have been able to reduce it
at once, but happily there was no resistance. On the contrary,
there was nothing but popular acclaim.

The airplanes, I think, were our most effective psychological
weapons. The daring manner in which our pilots buzzed the principal centers of population not only discouraged resistance but
actually encouraged support. It was difficult for the Egyptians
who watched them skimming over the rooftops not to feel a
sense of pride and exultation.

The only people who might have had a legitimate cause for
worry were the national and religious minorities whose need for
protection had served the British as a pretext for intervention in
the past. This was why we had taken precautions to prevent the
sort of bloody disorders that had made it possible for the British
to quell the Wafdists in 1919 as they had quelled the Orabists in
1882. This was why we had gone out of our way to inform the
American Embassy of the general purposes of our movement.
This was why I had reassured the foreigners in my proclamation,
and why I would reassure them in my speeches, that they would
be treated as brothers whose lives, interests, and property would
be respected. We were determined to give the British no excuse
whatever for acting against us as they had acted against our
revolutionary predecessors in the past.

x

Now that the first phase of our almost bloodless revolt had been
completed, it was time to begin Phase Two. Sadát, who knew
him better than the rest of us, was delegated to ask Ali Maher

if he would be willing to become the Free Officers' candidate to succeed Hilali as Prime Minister. Other officers were delegated to approach other politicians in the hope of finding an alternative candidate if Maher proved unwilling to associate himself with the military movement. In the meantime Hilali had offered to support the movement and to confirm my appointment as Commander in Chief on condition that we proclaim our fealty to the King. I put him off by saying that I was preparing another radio statement that I hoped would be acceptable to everyone concerned. We had already decided, of course, to replace Hilali with a Prime Minister who would be willing to do our bidding. I was relieved to learn a few minutes later that Maher had agreed to represent us. It seemed to me at the time that he was the only Egyptian politician who was qualified to do what needed to be done. Having known Faruk from childhood, having placed him on the throne, and having served as his chief of cabinet as well as his Prime Minister in the past, it was only fitting, I thought, that Maher should now assist us, wittingly or not, in dethroning his former protégé. No question of loyalty was involved. The King had so often betrayed him that Maher owed him nothing but contempt.

While I was preparing my statement a host of supplicants had gathered outside the Headquarters Building. Among them was a man named Sadek, whom I received in the mistaken impression that he was Fuad Sadek, the husband of Princess Faika. He turned out to be one of Narriman's uncles, Mustafa Sadek, who asked me to place an airplane at the disposal of the King and Queen. The King already had thirteen airplanes, including a C-47 that had been presented to him by the United States Air Force during the war. His chief pilot, Hassan Akef, who had gone to Almaza Field to prepare the C-47 for flight, had been refused admittance by our guards. Sadek had therefore come to see me in the hope of learning our intentions. I told him that since the lives of the King and Queen were not in danger there would be no reason for them to leave the country. I also told him that I intended to visit the King in Alexandria. Some of the officers wanted to arrest Sadek then and there, but I dissuaded them from doing so on the ground that it would be foolish to alarm the King unnecessarily.

At 11 A.M. I asked Sadát to broadcast the following statement:

"Egypt has been passing through a trying period of corruption and insecurity, which has had a profound effect upon the Army. Selfish and corrupt elements caused the Army's defeat in the Palestinian War. After the war was over, traitors conspired against the Army and left Egypt without any protection whatever. This is why the Army has decided to purge itself and put the affairs of our country in the hands of men whom we can trust.

"I have no doubt that the Egyptian people will welcome what we have done. As for the officers whom we have arrested, no harm will befall them. They will be released at the first opportune moment. The Army is working for the good of the country under the Constitution and has no selfish designs.

"I ask the people not to allow any traitors to resort to sabotage or violence, for such behavior will be against the interests of Egypt and will be severely punished. The Army, as I have previously announced, will perform its duties in co-operation with the police. Once again, I want to assure our foreign brothers that their interests will be respected. I consider myself personally responsible for their welfare."

Escorted by three armored cars, I then drove through the city to inspect the disposition of our forces. Everywhere I was greeted with applause. The people in the streets were as friendly as they could be. There was no sign of fear or resentment anywhere. It was obvious that the great majority of the people were on our side.

On my way back to GHQ, I visited the prisoners whom we were holding at the Military Academy in Abbassía. I shook hands with each of the prisoners in turn, answered questions, and promised to release them all as soon as I possibly could. A few of them grumbled, but most of them accepted their predicament philosophically. Some of them even congratulated me on the success of our coup d'état. They all laughed when my brother Ali and I shook hands.

Later in the day we would release all but thirty-four of the 236 political prisoners at Camp Huckstep, a former American barracks near what was then called Faruk Field, which had earlier been called Payne Field, and which is now called the Cairo International Airport. The thirty-four prisoners whom we continued to hold were persons who had been indicted for violating the law, which we still enforce, forbidding any sort of Communist activity in Egypt. The majority of those whom we released were persons who had been acquitted of the charges against them but who had been rearrested by Maraghi in order to prevent them from conspiring against the Hilali government. Although they included Socialists, Nationalists, and members of the Moslem Brotherhood, there were no known Communists among them.

XI

By the time I returned to GHQ, Hilali and his cabinet had resigned and the King had expressed his willingness to accept Maher as the new Prime Minister.

At 3 P.M., with several of my colleagues, I called on Maher at his home. After exchanging congratulations and consuming some lemonade and sandwiches, I informed him of the demands that we wanted him to present to the King as the conditions of his accepting office in our name. Haidar was to be dismissed and I was to succeed him as Commander in Chief of the Armed Forces. The executive committee of the Free Officers was to be responsible, for the time being, for all decisions affecting the security of Egypt. He, Maher, was to act as Minister of War, Interior, and Foreign Affairs, until we could find the right men to fill these posts. With these exceptions, I said, he would be free to choose his own cabinet so long as he selected men who were prepared to assist us in attaining our objectives. These included a purge of every ministry and political party, the prosecution of all grafters, regardless of their political affiliations, and a series of drastic social and economic reforms designed to improve the lot of the Egyptian people as a whole. Maher himself had long been urging a land reform, and we thought (mistakenly, as it developed) that he would be willing to sponsor the sort of reforms that we had in mind. In answer to his leading questions about our ultimate intentions, I hinted that we were thinking of making him the President of a future Egyptian Republic. In the meantime, I said, we would expect him to insist on the dismissal of all the King's advisers, official and unofficial, from Hafez Afifi down to Mohammed Hassan, the valet. Maher said that he would be only too glad to do so. We left him on the understanding that he would leave for Alexandria the following morning and that he would take office only if the King accepted our demands.

Back at GHQ we began to discuss the third phase of the coup d'état—the dethronement of the King. It took us until midnight to agree on the following plan: Zakaria Mohi ed Din, with two other officers, would proceed to Alexandria. As soon as Maher and his new cabinet had been installed in the government's summer quarters at Bulkeley, Mohi ed Din was to lay siege to either or both of the King's palaces—Montazah, at the eastern end of the beach, on the road to Abu Kir, or Ras el Tin, on the lighthouse promontory, facing the western harbor. Twenty-six tanks and armored cars, a battery of field artillery, and a battalion of motorized infantry would be sent to Alexandria in time to carry out either or both attacks at five o'clock on the evening of July 25. In the meantime, while the Navy patrolled the coast, the Air Force would patrol the sky. An ultimatum would be delivered to the King as soon as his palaces had been surrounded. The attack or attacks would then begin or not, depending on Faruk's reaction to our ultimatum.

There was no time for us to sleep that night or the next night either. Five successive nights, in fact, would pass before any of us had time for more than a nap. Precautions had to be taken in Cairo and Alexandria to prevent possible sabotage, and even greater precautions had to be taken in the Canal Zone to delay, if not to prevent, a possible British invasion.

The King, as we would learn, had already asked the American ambassador to inform the British that he urgently desired their help. Caffery had demurred on the ground that his government was opposed to foreign intervention. He had promised, however, to protect the lives of the King and his family if the need to do so should arise. But Faruk was not satisfied with Caffery's promise to save his life. He appealed to General Sir William Slim, the then commander of British Troops in Egypt, to smuggle him out of Egypt together with all his entourage. When Slim demurred, Faruk asked him to occupy Cairo and to request the British Navy, if necessary, to bombard Alexandria. Both of Faruk's appeals, which we intercepted, were transmitted by radio from Montazah Palace to the British GHQ in the Canal Zone. The second appeal was referred to Anthony Eden in London, and Eden in turn referred it to Dean Acheson in Washington. Acheson, after consulting President Truman, informed Eden that the United States Government would strongly oppose any thought of foreign intervention in the circumstances. It was only then that the British Government decided to ignore Faruk's second appeal.

Early in the morning of Thursday, July 24, I saw Maher off on the train to Alexandria. I approved the names of the men he intended to appoint to his cabinet and reminded him once again that we would expect him to purge the palace as well as the various ministries.

That afternoon I held my first press conference—or conferences, rather, for the first was in Arabic for local and regional journalists and the second in English for the foreign journalists who could not speak Arabic. The questions asked by both groups indicated that our enemies were accusing us of being at one and the same time Communists, Moslem Brothers, and self-seeking military adventurers. Some of the journalists also suspected that we were about to dethrone the King.

By evening the air was so full of rumors that I broadcast another radio message addressed, as before, "To my brothers, the sons of the Nile":

"It gives me great pleasure to address you again, despite the heavy burdens that I have assumed in the present delicate circumstances. I am talking to you personally in order to dispel the malicious rumors being spread by your enemies, the enemies of Egypt, about the military movement which has had your blessing from its inception.

"The movement has no personal aims; it seeks the advantage of no individual. Its only purpose is to introduce reforms and to purge the Army and the government of evildoers and thus restore respect for the Constitution.

"Inasmuch as weaklings are still spreading biased reports about the movement, I want to take this opportunity to assure you that it has been a success and that my colleagues and I are prepared for all eventualities.

"We are going forward with the faith and strength that your support has given us. Do not listen to rumors. Go forward with us in defense of the Army, in defense of Egypt.

"May the Almighty guide our steps and purify our hearts to the end that Egypt may once again attain a position worthy of its name."

XII

On Friday, July 25, I flew to Alexandria to carry out the third and last phase of the coup d'état. Half the committee joined me in my temporary headquarters in the barracks at Mustafa Pasha; the other half remained in Cairo with Abd el Nasser at the Headquarters Building in Kubri el Kubba. Operation Dethronement was scheduled to begin at 5 P.M. One hour later I was to meet the Prime Minister at the Government Building in Bulkeley to request him to deliver our ultimatum to the King.

In the late afternoon, however, when we assembled to discuss our final plans, Zakaria Mohi ed Din requested us to postpone the operation until five o'clock the following morning. We were reluctant to do so, but the reasons he gave us were sound. Some of our tanks had broken down on the Desert Road and would not reach Alexandria until late that night. They would be needed if the Royal Guards at either palace attempted to resist our siege. Our soldiers, who had gone without sleep for two nights, were beginning to complain of fatigue. They would fight better—if it came to a fight—if we let them have some rest. The King, more-over, had disappeared—or at least he had eluded the spies whom we had assigned to observe his movements. In the early hours of the morning, Faruk and his family had left Montazah and driven westward in the direction of Alexandria in one of his many Cadil-lacs. Faruk himself was at the wheel. He had driven so rapidly that our spies in their jeeps had lost sight of the Cadillac as it sped through Bulkeley. He was now believed to be at Ras el Tin, but it was always possible that he had gone into hiding with his family in his lavish apartment in the Moassat Hospital.

After a long discussion we authorized Mohi ed Din to postpone the dethronement operation for another twelve hours. One of our number flew back to Cairo to inform the others of our decision. Sadát went to see Maher to tell him that I would be unable to meet him until eight o'clock the following morning. The Prime Minister himself had been out of touch with the King since early the night before. Sadát did his best to allay his suspicions, but Maher told us later that he had already learned from Nagumi, Faruk's military aide, that the King had gone into hiding in the expectation that the British would intervene in time to keep him on his throne.

At 9 P.M., after Sadát had returned from Bulkeley, we as-sembled again to consider what to do with the King if he accepted our ultimatum. Should we arrest him and place him on trial with his cronies, or should we send him into exile? We couldn't afford to free him and let him remain in Egypt, for his supporters would be sure to plot against us. Gamál Salem was in favor of trying the

King for his crimes. Some of the others agreed with me that it would be enough to banish him from Egypt. A King, whatever his crimes, should not be placed on trial. Neither should he be imprisoned, I said, for then it would look as if we ourselves were criminals.

"No!" said Salem in a loud voice. "We stand for justice and we must see that justice is done. We can't afford to let him go."

"Our Revolution," said one of the others, "has been almost bloodless, thanks to our effort to keep it pure. Why spoil its purity by spilling blood—even Faruk's blood—if it isn't absolutely necessary?"

"Remember Faruk's victims," said Salem. "Remember the martyrs in Palestine who died because of Faruk's defective arms. It is our duty to avenge them."

"I'm not interested in whether Faruk should be punished or not," I said. "I'm interested only in the future of Egypt. If it will help Egypt to kill Faruk, then we must kill him. If it will help Egypt not to kill him, then we must let him go. Our task is not to seek vengeance; our task is to liberate the Egyptian people."

The debate continued for three hours. At the end of all that time we were still divided. Finally I stopped the argument.

"After all," I said, "we're only half the committee. The other half are in Cairo. Let's ask them what they think."

I looked at my watch. It was then midnight. Only five hours remained. It would be foolish to try to discuss the matter by telephone, for it was much too important.

Turning to Salem, I said, "Gamál, you fly up to Cairo. Tell Abd el Nasser and the others about our argument. I know you think that Faruk should be executed, but I also know that you're a man of integrity. We'll trust you to give a fair report."

Salem promised to do so, saying that he was sure a majority of those in Cairo would be in favor of execution.

It was four-thirty before he returned.

"You win," he said. "The others agree with you."

He handed me a written statement from Abd el Nasser expressing their point of view. I read it aloud:

"The Liberation Movement should get rid of Faruk as quickly as possible in order to deal with what is more important—namely, the need to purge the country of the corruption that Faruk will leave behind him. We must pave the way toward a new era in which the people will enjoy their sovereign rights and live in dignity. Justice is one of our objectives. We cannot execute Faruk without a trial. Neither can we afford to keep him in jail and preoccupy ourselves with the rights and wrongs of his case at the risk of neglecting the other purposes of the Revolution. Let us spare Faruk and send him into exile. History will sentence him to death."

I have never felt greater admiration for Abd el Nasser than I felt at that moment.

At 5 A.M., after the last of our tanks and armored cars had arrived from Cairo, I ordered our forces to surround both palaces as quietly as possible. We had meanwhile ascertained that Faruk was not at the Moassat Hospital. He was almost certainly at Ras el Tin, but, for fear that he might return to Montazah by boat, we decided to take no chances.

At seven I gave the order to attack. The Royal Guards at Montazah surrendered after firing a few token volleys into the air. We knew then that the King was still at Ras el Tin, where the Royal Guards might also have surrendered after a few token volleys if one of our junior officers had not misunderstood his orders. Instead of following the armored car that was to have provided them with cover, he and his men raced ahead of it in the direction of the *haramlik*. They had almost reached the entrance when the Royal Guards opened fire with their machine guns. The officer and his men replied, and for several minutes there was a lively exchange of fire. Then, realizing his mistake, the officer ordered his men to hold their fire, and, as soon as they had done so, the Royal Guards did the same.

This one skirmish was the only resistance that we encountered. Faruk's subsequent account of how our soldiers fired at him and his daughters and how he returned their fire from one of the harem balconies was pure fiction. So was his account of how the princesses "discovered the bodies of their pet dogs slain by the Naguibists in the stable." The only casualties at Ras el Tin were human beings, and they were the victims of the mistake that I have just described. Exactly six men were wounded. They were the only casualties suffered by man or beast in the Alexandria area. Counting the casualties suffered in the Cairo area, they made a grand total of ten—two dead and eight wounded. We regretted, of course, that there had been any casualties at all, for we had done our best to carry out a bloodless coup d'état. Even so, I think we can take some pride in the fact that the casualties were as low as they were. Few if any revolutions, I think, have accomplished more with the loss of fewer lives.

XIII

At 8 A.M. I went to the Government Building at Bulkeley to request the Prime Minister to deliver our ultimatum to the King. I was accompanied by Suleiman Hafez, the vice-president of the Council of State, which is the Egyptian equivalent of the American Supreme Court. Hafez assisted me in drafting our ultimatum. He also assisted me in drafting the act of abdication that we would force the King to sign.

The Prime Minister was not in his office when we arrived. The King had summoned him to Ras el Tin, which by then had been occupied by our forces. When Maher finally appeared at nine-twenty it was unnecessary to acquaint him with what had happened. All we had to do was to hand him our ultimatum:

"From Lieutenant General Mohammed Naguib Bey, Commander in Chief, to King Faruk:

"Whereas corruption has spread throughout the country as the result of your repeated violations of the Constitution and your complete disregard of the will of the people, who have lost confidence in the administration of justice and in public security and honor;

"And whereas you have thereby damaged the reputation of Egypt in the eyes of other countries;

"And whereas you have condoned the bribery and treachery revealed in consequence of our defeat in the Palestinian War;

"I, Mohammed Naguib, in the name of the Army, which represents the will of the people, have been authorized to demand that you abdicate in favor of your son, Prince Ahmed Fuad II, before 1200 and that you leave this country forever before 1800 today.

"If you refuse to comply with this ultimatum, you will be held responsible for the consequences."

Hafez and I returned to Mustafa Pasha while Maher went to Ras el Tin to deliver the ultimatum. At ten-thirty the first secretary of the American Embassy, Joseph S. Sparks, came to see me. He told me that his ambassador had been requested by the Secretary of State in Washington to inform the Prime Minister that the United States Government was prepared to regard the coup d'état as an internal matter of direct concern to Egyptians only. At the same time, he said, the United States Government hoped that the situation would not get out of hand. Caffery would therefore welcome some assurance from me that, whatever happened, no harm would befall the King or any member of his family and that they would be allowed to leave Egypt "with honor." I told Sparks that he could assure his ambassador that the situation was well in hand and that, so long as the King behaved himself, neither he nor any member of his family would be harmed.

While I was talking to Sparks I received a telephone call from one of our officers at Ras el Tin. The ambassador's personal secretary, Robert Simpson, had driven up in his car and was trying to force his way through the cordon of troops surrounding the palace. He was determined to see the King. I told the officer to let him pass. Maher told me later that he was talking to Faruk in one of the reception halls when Simpson appeared in the corridor outside.

"Come in, come in," said the King. "I've never been so glad to see anyone in my life. We haven't much time. I have just two things to tell your ambassador. Ask him if he will do what he can to save my life. If he does, will he come to say good-by? They're making me abdicate at twelve and leave the country at six."

Simpson delivered the message to Caffery, who called at the palace at eleven-thirty to inform Faruk that I had promised to allow him and his family to leave Egypt in safety and with honor. Hafez and I had meanwhile rejoined the Prime Minister at Bulkeley. Maher returned the ultimatum, which Faruk had countersigned, and informed us that the King would abdicate in favor of his son, Ahmed Fuad II, provided: (1) that the act of abdication be worded in a dignified manner; (2) that he be allowed to sail to Naples aboard the *Mahroussa*, the royal yacht on which he had squandered so much of the people's money; (3) that he be given a royal salute of twenty-one guns as he boarded the *Mahroussa;* and (4) that I should attend his departure. Although Faruk was in no position to bargain, I agreed to accept his conditions in return for one of my own—that the *Mahroussa,* as the property of the Egyptian people, be sent back to Alexandria as soon as Faruk and his party had disembarked at Naples.

Inasmuch as the Prime Minister was to receive the American ambassador at twelve-thirty, it was Hafez who went to Ras el Tin at one to present the following act of abdication:

"We, Faruk Fuad I, desiring the welfare, happiness, and advancement of our country, and wishing to help it overcome the difficulties with which it is faced in the present delicate circumstances, have decided, in accordance with the will of the people, to abdicate in favor of our son, Crown Prince Ahmed Fuad II.

"We hereby authorize His Excellency Ali Maher, President of the Council of Ministers, to proceed in accordance with this act."

Faruk, after reading the document, asked if it was entirely legal. Hafez assured him that it was. He then wanted to strike out the phrase "in accordance with the will of the people," but Hafez finally persuaded him to sign the act as it was written. His hand was trembling so badly that his first signature was almost illegible. Although Hafez assured him that it would not be necessary, he insisted on signing the document again. His second signature was much clearer than his first.

Faruk then asked Hafez to do what he could to make it possible for Pulli and Mohammed Hassan to accompany him into exile. He also asked to be allowed to retain his costly collections of coins and postage stamps. Hafez duly transmitted these requests. At first we were inclined to let him keep his coins and stamps, but, remembering the large sums of currency that he had been smuggling out of Egypt, we finally decided to confiscate all of his property except his clothing, jewelry, and personal effects. We later sold his property at a series of public auctions and used the proceeds to finance our reforms. As for Pulli and Mohammed Hassan, we reasoned that if we let them go we would have to let the others go; and, if we let all of the King's retainers go, how could we possibly hope to restore a sense of public morality in Egypt? Justice should be tempered with mercy, but there is a point beyond which mercy becomes injustice. We could afford to let the King escape because he represented something above and beyond himself. To have tried him would have meant trying the Mohammed Ali dynasty, not all of whose representatives had been evil or worthless men, and to have tried the dynasty would have meant trying the political institutions of modern Egypt, which we had no desire to do. Faruk, however, was the only exception that we could afford to make. All of his cronies whom we could capture would have to be tried impartially for their crimes. Otherwise the Revolution would lose the popular support on which its legitimacy depended.

Narriman's mother, Assila Sadek, and two of Faruk's five sisters, Faiza and Fawzía, and their husbands, came to the palace to attend the former King's departure. Fathía and Fawkía were in the United States with the former Queen Nazli, whom Faruk himself had banished from Egypt, and Faika and her husband had gone to Finland to attend the Olympic Games. Faruk had dressed for the occasion in the uniform of an Egyptian admiral. The only other persons who were present, aside from a few officers and the palace servants, were the Prime Minister, the American ambassador, and the latter's secretary, Robert Simpson.

Narriman, who was dressed in a traveling suit, was the first to descend to the palace quay. She was followed by Crown Prince

Ahmed Fuad, carried in the arms of his British nurse, and by Faruk's three daughters by his former wife—Ferial, Fawzía, and Fadia. According to a journalist who appears to have taken the trouble to count them, they were accompanied by 204 pieces of baggage. Then Faruk, dressed in his admiral's uniform, descended to the quay. The royal standard dipped and the palace band played the national anthem as he stepped aboard the cutter that was to carry him out to the *Mahroussa,* which was anchored in the roadstead. The palace servants, in accordance with Egyptian custom, set up a wail of lament that could be heard a quarter of a mile away. It was punctuated by the rhythmic booming of the twenty-one-gun salute.

Accompanied by Gamál Salem and several other officers, including Captain (now Major) Ismail Faríd, who was to become my secretary, I arrived at the quay too late to take leave of Faruk before he boarded the *Mahroussa.* We had been held up by cheering crowds of demonstrators in Alexandria, and our driver, instead of taking us directly to the quay, took us to the opposite side of the palace. When we finally reached the quay, I ordered a cutter to take us out to the *Mahroussa,* but its pilot, not realizing that we intended to board the ship, circled round her instead of taking us up to the jacob's ladder where two seamen were waiting to make us fast.

At last we tied up at the bottom of the ladder and clambered aboard the ship. Faruk was waiting for us on the bridge. I saluted him and he returned my salute. A long and embarrassing pause ensued. Neither of us knew what to say. We were both gripped by a mixture of emotions that brought us close to tears.

"Effendim," I said at last, addressing him politely as a private citizen rather than a king, "you remember that I was the only Egyptian officer who submitted his resignation in 1942."

"Yes, I remember," said Faruk.

"I was ashamed of the humiliation to which the King of Egypt had been subjected."

"I know."

"We were loyal to the throne in 1942, but many things have changed since then."

"Yes, I know. Many things have changed."

"It was you, *effendim,* who forced us to do what we have done."

Faruk's reply will puzzle me for the rest of my life.

"I know," he said. "You've done what I always intended to do myself."

I was so surprised that I could think of nothing more to say. I saluted and the others did likewise. Faruk returned our salutes and we all shook hands.

"I'm sorry not to have received you at the quay," he said, "but you ordered me to be out of Egypt by six o'clock. I kept my word."

We nodded and prepared to leave the bridge. But Faruk had not yet finished.

"I hope you'll take good care of the Army," he said. "My grandfather, you know, created it."

"The Egyptian Army," I said, "is in good hands."

"Your task will be difficult. It isn't easy, you know, to govern Egypt. . . ."

Such were Faruk's last words. I felt sorry for him as we disembarked. Faruk, I knew, would fail as an exile even as he had failed as a king. But he was such an unhappy man in every way that I could take no pleasure in his destitution, necessary though it was.

No, it would not be easy to govern Egypt, but the task would be less difficult for us than Faruk had made it for himself. We were prepared to face our responsibilities, which was something that Faruk had never attempted to do, and we were at one with the Egyptian people, to whom Faruk, like his father before him, had always been a stranger. For the first time in modern history, Egypt would have a government, in Lincoln's words, that would be "of the people, by the people, and for the people."

It was that thought which encouraged us then, and which still encourages us, despite the differences that have grown up between us, in our effort to lead the Egyptian people toward a prosperous new era of social justice and economic co-operation.

4

THE REVOLUTION

On Monday, July 28, we moved the seat of government back to Cairo. For years the government had been wasting time and money trying to do its work in Alexandria during the five hot summer months. It was time, we thought, for the politicians and bureaucrats to realize that they were the servants, not the masters, of the Egyptian people. We had no objection to their visiting Alexandria as individuals and at their own expense, over week ends and during their vacations, but we objected to their traveling back and forth between Cairo and Alexandria in the summertime at the expense of the Egyptian taxpayer. If the people of Cairo could stand the heat, why shouldn't their civil servants, as they liked to call themselves, be made to stand it too?

The Government Building in Bulkeley was accordingly evacuated and turned over to the overcrowded University of Alexandria, as it was now to be called, instead of Faruk University, as it had been called in the past. The name of the larger of the two

universities in Cairo was similarly changed from Fuad University
to the University of Cairo. Cairo's second university, to which we
have since presented Za'afaran Palace, is still named for Ibrahim
Pasha, the best of the dynasty founded by his father, Mohammed
Ali.

All of the King's cronies who were still in Egypt were arrested
and placed on trial. Sirri Amer, who was captured while attempting to escape to Libya in a stolen automobile, was eventually convicted and sentenced to life imprisonment. Karím Tabet was also
sentenced to life imprisonment. Serag ed Din was sentenced to
fifteen years' imprisonment, as were many other convicted grafters,
including Abbas Halím, whose sentence was suspended.

All but three of the officers whom we arrested at the time of
the coup d'état were soon released. So were 264 persons who had
been arrested on charges of complicity in the burning of Cairo.
We eventually decreed an amnesty providing pardons, on condition of future good behavior, for all persons, including Communists, who had been convicted of political crimes and misdemeanors prior to July 23, 1952. We wanted to wipe the slate
clean and begin all over again. We retained the anti-Communist
law, however, along with other laws designed to protect the state.
Although many of the persons whom we released have had to be
rearrested for committing new crimes and misdemeanors, I think
that we can truthfully say that we gave every political prisoner a
fair chance to resume normal life under the new regime. There has
been no political persecution and there will be no political persecution in Egypt so long as I am in a position to prevent it.

We have also done our best to prevent the resurgence of
nepotism. One of my first acts following the King's dethronement
was to rescind the decree by which I had been promoted to the
rank of lieutenant general and granted the salary of a minister.

Although I remained the Commander in Chief of the Armed Forces until Amer succeeded me in that position, I resumed the rank and continued to receive the salary of a major general until I succeeded Ali Maher as Prime Minister.[1] I allowed my brother Ali to become the Egyptian ambassador to Syria because he was one of nine senior officers whose services outside of the Army my colleagues wanted to retain. Colonel Adib Shishakli and his military group were then in control of the Syrian Government and it was only logical for our own military government to be represented in Syria by a senior officer. Ali, moreover, was the man best qualified to fill the post, for he had served for ten years as the Egyptian military secretary to the British Governor General of Sudan. My sister Naguía was offered a fellowship to complete her pediatric studies in the United States and my brother Mahmúd was offered a fellowship to complete his veterinary studies in England. I did my best to prevent them both from accepting these honors, even though they honestly deserved them, for I knew that they and I would be subject to criticism if they did. I succeeded with Naguía but I failed with Mahmúd. Naguía decided to be married and remain in Egypt instead of going to the United States. Mahmúd, however, insisted on taking advantage of the opportunity that was offered him to obtain his doctorate in veterinary pharmacology at Guy's Medical College in London. I twice blocked his appointment, but the second time he filed suit against the Ministry of Education to show why he should not be allowed to accept the fellowship. There was nothing to do but let him have his way, for, as an honor student, he would have won the fellowship on a competitive basis if I had not interfered.

---

[1]The comparative salaries were as follows: Ministers (including the Prime Minister), LE 2500 ($7175); Lieutenant Generals, LE 1500 ($4305); Major Generals, LE 1200 ($3444).

As for the rest of my associates, only one has been exceptionally promoted since the coup d'état. Amer, in order to succeed me as Commander in Chief, was promoted to the rank of major general and has since been paid the salary of a minister.

On July 30 we abolished the official titles of bey and pasha and the unofficial title of His Excellency. Until that date, Ali Maher, like all Prime Ministers, had been a pasha, just as I, like all major generals, had been a bey. These titles, which were of Turkish origin, were not hereditary; they were merely honors bestowed by the King on Egyptians and Sudanese who had attained positions in society that were judged to be worthy of recognition. They were bestowed on men of humble as well as exalted origin. Usually they went with a man's job or with his wealth. If he was moderately successful, he usually became a bey; if he was extremely successful he usually became a pasha. But not always, for the titles depended on the pleasure of an abnormal King who often bestowed them on people who did not deserve them. Andraos, for example, had become a pasha; Pulli had become a bey; and Mohammed Hilmi Hussein, the King's chauffeur, had become at once a bey and an honorary brigadier.

It took us some time to put a stop to the use of titles, but we finally succeeded, in spite of the fact that the habit of flattering individuals by calling them beys and pashas, even if they had no titles, was deeply rooted in a people who had long been accustomed to despotic rule. Another difficulty arose from the fact that there is no satisfactory equivalent for "mister" in the Arabic language. *"Hadret"* was the nearest equivalent, but it was not polite enough to come naturally to Egyptians. We finally settled for *"el sayed,"* which is the equivalent of "master," as indeed "mister" was in the beginning. (The same word is also applied to descendants of the Prophet.) Perhaps in time we can do away with appellatives altogether, which would be more in accordance with the austerity of the Islamic faith, but for the present *"el sayed"* is the best that we can do.

So many people continued to call me "bey," even after we had officially abolished the use of titles, that I began to fine them a piaster every time they used the word in my presence. Others followed my example, and before long even servants began to realize that we were in earnest. But the habit was so hard to break that, on one occasion, I was fined myself for referring to Ali Maher as "His Excellency." Instead of paying a piaster, I paid two piasters, since the use of "Excellency," in my opinion, was twice as bad as the use of "bey" or "pasha."

II

Although Faruk had abdicated in favor of his son, Ahmed Fuad II, Egypt obviously could not be ruled by an infant whom we had allowed to be carried into exile. Most of my younger colleagues would have preferred to declare Egypt a republic right away, but I persuaded them to do as the Prime Minister suggested and appoint a Council of Regents to represent the King. The regency would disarm our monarchist enemies and give us time to prepare the people for the republic that would eventually replace the monarchy. It would also give Rashad Mehanna something to do until we could find a better place for him.

Mehanna, who was by then a full colonel, felt that we owed him an important job. In a sense we did, for he had co-operated with the Free Officers; but he was so deeply involved with the Moslem Brothers that we could not afford to make him a member of the executive committee. He resented the failure of his own revolutionary efforts and begrudged us the success of ours. He objected, moreover, to our unanimous desire to make Egypt a secular republic. What he wanted, and what most of the Moslem Brothers wanted, was to go back to the days of the Sultan Saláh ed Din when Egypt was a theocratic state. The rest of us, while sympathizing with the desire to apply the teachings of Mohammed to modern life, were convinced that to do so blindly would spell disaster. The rebirth of Egypt, in our opinion, depended on the continued modernization of its social, political, and economic institutions.

Egypt is the melting pot of the Middle East. Such prosperity as it has enjoyed in modern times has been largely due to its ability to attract and absorb foreigners and assimilate their ideas. There is nothing in the Koran that calls for theocratic government; on the contrary, the Prophet was in favor of parliamentary rule. By urging believers to decide their affairs "by counsel among themselves," he made it clear that God wished Moslems to govern themselves within the kingdom of His faith and to respect "those who fight you not for religion's sake." It is thus not only permissible but desirable for a cosmopolitan country like Egypt to be governed by means of a secular republic in which the rights of minorities shall be respected so long as the minorities, in turn, respect the Islamic way of life.

This does not mean that my colleagues and I have chosen to turn our backs on the Islamic faith. On the contrary, we hope to strengthen the faith by applying its teachings judiciously rather than blindly, as some groups in Egypt would have us do. The theory behind Islamic law is as good as any and better than most, in my opinion, but because fanatics have been so prone to misinterpret the law it has been assumed by many that it is inconsistent with the conditions of modern life. This is a mistake. The injunctions of the Koran have as much meaning and application today as they ever did, provided they are interpreted with due regard for the many changes that have occurred in human society since the Prophet preached his message.

The question of polygamy is a case in point. "Marry such women as seem good to you," the Koran says, "two, or three, or four. But if you fear that you will not do justice, then [marry] only one. . . . This is more proper that you may not do injustice." Again, referring to the same subject, the Koran says, "And you cannot do justice between wives, even though you wish [it], but be not disinclined [from one] with total disinclination, so that you leave her in suspense. And if you are reconciled and keep your duty, surely Allah is ever Forgiving, Merciful."

In order to interpret these verses correctly, it is necessary to compare the conditions of life among the Arabs in the seventh century, when Mohammed preached his message, with the conditions of life among the Moslem peoples today. The people whom Mohammed converted to Islam were pagan, polygamous, illiterate, and decimated by years of civil war. There was a great surplus of women and orphans and a great need for more male children in order to guarantee the survival of the various tribes. It would have been difficult indeed for Mohammed to convert such people to Islam if he had blindly forbidden polygamy in the face of established custom and biological necessity. He confined himself therefore to gentle opposition. He permitted men to take up to four wives, provided they could do them justice. At the same time he assured them that they could not do justice to more than one.

Today the practice of polygamy is disappearing among all the Moslem peoples except the beduin and the more retarded peasantry. As we improve the conditions of life among the peasants of Egypt, they, too, will cease to be polygamous; and so will the

beduin once they have been offered the means of leading a settled
life. In the meantime, so long as it serves its purpose, I consider
polygamy preferable to the promiscuity and prostitution that exist
in certain Western countries where two World Wars have tended
to create a surplus of women. In Germany, I believe, polygamy
has been seriously advocated as the only sensible solution to the
problem.

III

At a press conference on July 30, I announced that Egypt, in
spite of the abolition of titles, would continue to be a constitutional monarchy. Unfortunately the Constitution of 1922, which
Faruk had suspended, made no provision for the King's abdication. It provided only that the Chamber of Deputies, which Faruk
had also suspended, should reconvene within ten days of the
King's death to appoint a Council of Regents if his heir was under
age. We were thus faced with the dilemma of reconvening the
Wafdist Chamber and running the risk of open dissension in the
midst of our Revolution or of leaving the Chamber in a state of
suspension and amending the suspended Constitution by executive decree.

Suleiman Hafez suggested that we refer our dilemma to the
Council of State. We did so, and the Council, meeting under the
presidency of Abd er Razak es Sanhuri, decided by a vote of nine
to one that there was no need, in the circumstances, to reconvene
the old Chamber of Deputies. A new Chamber of Deputies would
have to be elected. In the meantime the Prime Minister had the
constitutional right, in the absence of any provision to the contrary and in accordance with the residual powers vested in his

office, to appoint a provisional Council of Regents until such time as a new Chamber of Deputies could meet to consider the problem.

The Constitution specified that the regents should be Egyptian Moslems selected from among the princes of the royal family and their close relatives, prime ministers and ministers, deputies, and senators. In order to make Mehanna a regent, therefore, it was necessary for Maher to appoint him Minister of Communications. The other two regents whom he appointed with our approval were Mohammed Bahi ed Din Barakát and Prince Mohammed Abd el Moneim.

The legality of the provisional Council of Regents was questionable, perhaps, but few if any Egyptians questioned our appointments. It was only logical that the Army should be represented, since the Army had carried out the Revolution, and in the beginning, at least, Mehanna seemed to be a worthy representative. Bahi ed Din Barakát was a former president of the Senate, had almost succeeded Sirri as Prime Minister, and was the best and most honest director of the State Audit Department that Egypt had ever had. Unfortunately, like Mehanna, he was inordinately sensitive to what he deemed to be affronts to his dignity and self-respect. The third and most co-operative member of the Council of Regents was Prince Abd el Moneim. A charming man in every way, Abd el Moneim, in spite of his fifty-three years, was Faruk's nephew twice removed. He was also third in line of succession to the throne. His father, Abbas Hilmi II, had been dethroned by the British on the outbreak of the First World War. Abd el Moneim's wife, the Princess Nassli Shah, was the daughter of Prince Omar Faruk, the heir presumptive to the non-existent throne of Turkey. Abd el Moneim was in Paris at the time of his appointment, and so we had to wait until he could fly back to

Cairo on August 5 to be sworn in by the Prime Minister as the senior member of the Council of Regents.

In the meantime we appointed a series of committees to purge the Armed Forces and the various civilian ministries of grafters, nepotists, and others who had proved themselves unworthy of public trust. Before the committees had finished their work, a year later, some eight hundred bureaucrats and one hundred Army, Navy, Air Force, and police officers had been removed. The least guilty were allowed to resign in order not to lose their pensions; the guiltier were discharged; and the guiltiest were later tried before the Tribunal of the Revolution. The bureaucrats who survived the purge were henceforth compelled to do a full day's work and to treat the public with the courtesy to which it was entitled— something that a good many of them had never done before.

Other committees were appointed to investigate specific scandals, including the arms and cotton scandals, the illegal sale of government lands, and the widespread evasion of income taxes. The illegal wealth of persons found guilty by the Graft Court and the Tribunal of the Revolution was confiscated and is now being spent on schools, hospitals, and low-cost housing projects. The penalties for tax evasion were stiffened and the tax rates increased to the point where the state could obtain the maximum revenue consonant with its policy of encouraging the investment of new foreign and domestic capital. The taxes on income, for example, now increase progressively from approximately 8.5 per cent on personal incomes of LE 1500 ($4305) to approximately 18 per cent on incomes of LE 10,000 ($28,700) and approximately 47 per cent on incomes of LE 50,000 ($143,500). And, what is more important, income taxes are now being paid. Whereas evasion used to be the general rule, collection is today the general rule because evaders know that they will be made to pay the penalty if they are caught. It is no longer possible to bribe the tax collector as a matter of course, for today he, too, knows that he will go to jail if he is caught. I don't mean to say that Egyptians have been converted into angels since the Revolution, but I do mean to say that Egyptians have begun to behave differently now that they know that their laws are being impartially enforced.

We have not prohibited gambling and drinking, as the Moslem Brothers would have had us do, but we have stiffened the laws controlling such practices to the point where no one can say any longer that they seriously menace public morals.

I wish I could say as much of our effort to minimize the traffic in drugs. The growing of narcotic plants in Egypt has been successfully prohibited because of the difficulty of concealing their cultivation in such a heavily populated country. The importation of drugs from neighboring countries has been prohibited with much less success, however, not only because of the difficulty of patrolling Egypt's enormous deserts but also because of the failure of our Arab neighbors to stamp out the growing of narcotic plants in their own countries and because, of late, Israel has been encouraging the smuggling of drugs in the hope of thus reducing Egypt's ability to resist its efforts to dominate the Middle East.

Nevertheless the penalties today are so severe and so rigorously enforced that I think I can safely say that it is now almost as difficult to obtain hashish (marihuana) in Cairo or Alexandria as it is in most Western cities. Today every Egyptian knows that if he is caught smoking hashish he will receive a sentence of up to fifteen years of hard labor. And the smugglers and peddlers know that if they are caught with hashish in their possession they will receive sentences ranging up to life imprisonment if theirs is a first offense, and up to death if they have previously been convicted. (The same penalties apply to all other drugs except alcohol.)

Some readers may think that these penalties are too severe, but I am convinced that there is no other way to reduce the drug traffic in Egypt to manageable proportions, especially in view of the encouragement that smugglers have been receiving from our enemies abroad. I am fully aware that drug addiction is a symptom of illness as well as a crime, but so is most other criminal behavior, including murder; and what is the drug traffic but gradual mass murder, or what is now called genocide? Someday it may be possible in Egypt to treat drug addicts in hospitals, but for the time being we feel that hard labor is the best and indeed the only possible solution.

Begging is another problem that we have tried to solve. Little by little we are establishing farms for the rehabilitation of child beggars and other delinquent children. We have failed, I am sorry to say, to eliminate begging altogether, but we have succeeded in reducing the evil, and we hope to reduce it further in the future.

Our other reforms, in addition to the building of schools, hospitals, and low-cost houses, include the installation of potable wells, cheap toilets, electricity, and clinics in the villages and the erection of public toilets and the opening of public gardens in the cities. But the most important of all, by far, are the agrarian reforms, on which the success or failure of the Egyptian Revolution will depend. I use the phrase "agrarian reforms" in the plural instead of "land reform" in the singular because the problem we must solve is a human problem that can be solved only by a continuing series of reforms designed to improve the lot of the Egyptian peasant.

IV

In 1798, when Egypt was invaded by Napoleonic France, it was a backward Turkish colony inhabited by 2,500,000 people who lived precariously off the produce of some 3,000,000 sparsely culti-vated acres along the banks of the Nile. Today, after a hun-dred and fifty-six years of Western influence, and seventy-two years of total or partial British occupation, Egypt is inhabited by 22,000,000 people who live precariously off the produce of some 6,000,000 intensively cultivated acres. In other words, twice as much land must now feed nine times as many people, and, even with excessive irrigation and excessive chemical fertilization, it simply cannot do so. Even though two or three million inhabitants of Cairo, Alexandria, and the other cities are living better than Egyptians have ever lived before, most of the remaining nine-teen or twenty millions have been reduced to the lowest standard of living that the civilized world has ever known.

It does no good to blame such conditions on the British or the other peoples of the West. Neither does it do any good to blame such conditions on the character of the Egyptian people. The only relevant facts are that such conditions exist and that we, the Egyptians, with or without foreign assistance, are the only people who can improve them.

How do we intend to do so?

First, by enforcing the new minimum-wage laws. It is now illegal to pay men a daily wage of less than eighteen piasters (fifty-two cents) and women and children a daily wage of less than ten piasters (twenty-nine cents) for agricultural labor. Before the Revolution, though many landowners paid a good deal more, the average daily wage for adult male farm laborers was eight and a half piasters (twenty-four cents). Yet the average daily cost of keeping three typical Egyptian farm animals alive was: donkeys, eight piasters (twenty-three cents); mules, twelve piasters (thirty-four cents); and water buffaloes, twenty-eight piasters (eighty cents).[2]

Second, by reducing all estates and plantations except those owned by reclamation companies to a legal maximum of 200 acres. This limit, we feel, is more than sufficient in a country where an acre of irrigated farmland is worth from LE 350 ($1004.50) to LE 1000 ($2870.00). Approximately 440,000 acres belonging to some 1700 landowners are being expropriated in return for thirty-year government bonds bearing annual interest at 3 per cent. Approximately 185,000 acres belonging to some 175 members of the royal family have been expropriated without compensation. During the agrarian phase of our ten-year plan, the land fund thus created will be divided into parcels of not less than two or more than five acres and sold to qualified peasants owning fewer than five acres of farmland. All peasants owning fewer than five acres, whether purchasers of expropriated land or not, have been obliged to join co-operatives. The co-operatives, which are supervised by the government, lend money at nominal rates of interest; provide seeds, fertilizers, animals, machinery, transportation, and storage facilities; control irrigation and methods of cultivation; combat insects and plant and animal diseases; market the crops of their members; and, in return for contributions, provide certain educational, medical, and social services.

[2]These figures are based on a study made by Dr. Ahmed Hussein, the president of the Felláh Society. Dr. Hussein, who is not to be confused with the agitator of the same name who was implicated in the burning of Cairo, is a former Minister of Social Affairs who is now the Egyptian ambassador to the United States.

The purpose of the land reform is thus social as well as economic. Its social purpose is to restore the *fellah's* faith in his ability to better himself by his own efforts in co-operation with other *fellahin*. Probably not more than 150,000 peasant proprietors representing 1,000,000 individuals will benefit directly from the redistribution of land. But a little is better than nothing, and though only a minority in every village is able to purchase additional land, the results, we think, will be worth while. The minority will provide us with the village leaders of tomorrow. Their children will be healthier than the children of today. It is they on whom we count to improve living standards by setting an example to their fellow villagers. In the meantime the government will provide the villages with schools, electric lights, clinics, social centers, and sanitary and recreational facilities, including potable wells, cheap toilets, bathhouses, playing fields, and places for listening to the radio and seeing films. We thus hope to arrest the ruinous migration from the villages to the towns and cities that has developed in recent years.

The realization of our hopes will depend on a number of factors, the most important of which is Egypt's rapidly increasing population. Every day there are a thousand more mouths to feed than there were the day before. Thus, before we can improve living standards, we must first arrest their decline. Contraception has been suggested as an answer to the problem of Egypt's runaway population. In spite of religious objections, Christian as well as Moslem, the Council of the Revolution favors the control of births by every accepted means. But birth control by means of contraception is hardly feasible in villages where homes lack running water, toilets, and electric lights. A more effective means of controlling births, we feel, is to provide the villages with the rudiments of modern civilization. The mere introduction of electric lights in

certain Indian villages has tended to reduce the rate of their increase in population. There is no reason to believe that the introduction of electric lights in Egyptian villages will not have the
same effect.

The economic purpose of the land reform is to divert the investment of capital from existing farms to the reclamation of new
land and the development of new commercial and industrial enterprises. Abd el Galíl el Emari, one of Egypt's leading economists,
and a former Minister of Finance, has explained the economic
aspects of the land reform as follows:

"In order to raise the standard of living it is necessary to attain
our economic maturity as soon as possible. The Egyptian economy
has suffered until now from an obstacle that has prevented its development—the tendency of the wealthy to invest their capital in
farmlands, the amount of which has not increased in proportion
to the demand. Farmlands in Egypt have always constituted a
more or less exclusive field for capital investment.

"The investment of capital in farmlands has not had the effect
of increasing their acreage because so few investors have been
willing to risk their capital in reclaiming barren lands. Their
preference has been for lands that would assure them an immediate return on their investment. This form of investment has not
created wealth; it has merely concentrated the wealth already
present. Thus Egyptian farmlands have become a bottomless pit,
absorbing the bulk of our capital.

"The increase in the value of farmlands has caused proprietors
to do everything in their power to obtain an income in proportion
to the price they have paid for their land. Proprietors who could
not increase their income by raising the prices of their produce,
given the fact that prices are subject to what the market will bear,
have still been able to increase their income by reducing expenses

without reducing output. The reduction of expenses has always been made at the cost of the wages paid to farm laborers.

"There are thus two essential factors at work: the tendency of investors to buy farmlands that will assure them an immediate return on their money, and the reduced purchasing power of farm laborers.

"These two factors have impeded economic development in the agricultural field by impeding the increase of cultivable acreage and in the industrial field by impeding the development of established industries and the creation of new industries. . . .

"The principal objectives of the land reform project are to direct new capital investment toward land reclamation and commercial and industrial enterprises. Increased investments will make it possible to increase wages and hence the purchasing power of the general public."

V

We waited almost seven weeks for Ali Maher and his civilian advisers to promulgate the land reform that we had promised to decree. On September 7, when he had still failed, in spite of repeated warnings, to approve the decree law, we took matters into our own hands and appointed a new cabinet with myself as its Prime Minister. Two days later, after a stormy meeting that lasted for eighteen hours, I promulgated the land reform with certain modifications recommended by Maher and his advisers.

Although we refused to raise the limit on agricultural holdings from 200 to 500 acres, as Maher and others desired, we relaxed the 200-acre provision to the extent of allowing owners of more than 200 acres to transfer, within five years, a maximum of 100 acres to their children, provided that no one child should receive more than fifty acres. We also authorized owners of more than 200 acres to sell five-acre parcels to owners of not more than ten acres, provided their family relationship with such persons was at least five times removed. The latter concession has had to be annulled. Too many landowners attempted to sell too many parcels of land to straw men who were simply their agents in disguise. The former provision has perhaps been justified even though it has reduced the land fund at our disposal from an estimated 735,000 acres to an estimated 625,000 acres. The 110,000 acres divided among the children of big landowners should make it possible for them to adjust themselves to the new regime without excessive hardship.

Many expropriated landowners complain that we have charged them too much in the form of taxes and paid them too little in the form of compensation. On all undistributed holdings of more than 200 acres we have imposed a special tax of five times the normal tax. Inasmuch as the usual income from agricultural land in Egypt, whether derived from rents, shares, or direct profits, is seven times the normal tax, the owner of more than 200 acres has been allowed to retain two sevenths of his normal income from surplus land until such land has been sold or expropriated or, in the case of the first 100 acres above 200, transferred to his children. The same landowner has been allowed to retain all of his income from his first 200 acres.

The average value of agricultural property in Egypt is seventy times the normal tax. Thus, if a person owns 200 acres worth LE 500 ($1435) each, his annual income before taxes will average one tenth of LE 100,000 ($287,000), or LE 10,000 ($28,700). If he owns 500 acres worth LE 500 each, of which he has transferred 100 to his children, 200 acres will be subject to expropriation. He is allowed to retain two sevenths of his annual income from such surplus acreage, or LE 2857 ($8200). His annual income until the day his land is expropriated, when it will revert to LE 10,000 ($28,700), will thus be LE 12,857, or $36,900.

On the day of expropriation the same landowner will receive as compensation government bonds to the value of seventy times the annual tax that he paid on his 200 surplus acres in 1944, or in the earliest taxable year thereafter, provided he acquired his surplus acreage later. Thus, if he paid a tax per acre of LE 10 ($28.70) in that year, he will receive 3 per cent bonds in the amount of LE 100,000 (287,000), which is the true value of his expropriated property. If, however, he undervalued his property and paid a tax of only LE 5 ($14.35), he will receive 3 per cent bonds in the amount of LE 50,000 ($143,500), which is only half the true value of the same acreage.

I shall leave it to the reader to decide whether or not it is just to compensate landowners who have paid their full taxes at the full value of their property and to compensate landowners who have not paid their full taxes in proportion to the taxes that they have actually paid.

Many criticisms of the land reform have been made by persons who have failed to understand that it is a means to an end and not an end in itself. We have made a lot of mistakes, none of them irrevocable, which we are now correcting with the help of native and foreign advisers, many of them American employees of the Technical Cooperation Administration, otherwise known as "Point Four." But, for all the mistakes we have made, I still feel that we did well to insist on a rapid if imperfect land reform. Had we waited to perfect the land reform, we might still be debating whether or not to promulgate the decree today. Politics is the art of the possible, and the possibilities grow less with every day that passes, particularly in the midst of a revolution.

Ali Maher and his friends would have preferred to achieve the results that we expect to achieve by means of confiscatory taxation rather than expropriation. We disagreed with them for several reasons, the most important of which is the psychological effect of distributing parcels of land among peasants who had lost hope of ever becoming landowners themselves. The land reform, as I have said, is but the first of a long series of agrarian reforms designed to raise the morale of the Egyptian people, 75 per cent of whom are peasants.

What better means is there of raising a peasant's morale, and thereby his initiative, than by making it possible for him to buy a piece of land? A landless peasant is a demoralized and defenseless person. A landed peasant is a man of spirit who will defend his land, if necessary, with his life. The difference between a landless and a landed peasant is the difference between a two-footed animal and a man. Too many Egyptian peasants have been reduced through the years to the level of two-footed animals. What Egypt needs for its renaissance is men, and we are counting on the agrarian reforms to help us to produce them.

Another criticism of our land reform is that we have given too much power to the government-controlled co-operatives. Our co-operative program is said to smack of authoritarianism. Perhaps it does, but who but the government in Egypt is able and willing to take the measures necessary to ensure the land reform's success? One reason why land reforms have failed in some countries is that no provisions were made to protect their beneficiaries from the moneylenders and swindlers who were waiting to exploit their lack of capital and experience. By obliging all peasants owning fewer than five acres to join co-operatives under government supervision, we have made it impossible for them to be so victimized. At the same time we have extended the technical benefits of the land reform to all who need them, regardless of whether or not they have purchased expropriated land.

It can be argued that compulsion and co-operation are contradictory concepts, and that co-operatives, ideally, should be voluntary associations. Given the deplorable conditions of life in Egyptian villages, however, the distinction between compulsion and co-operation is irrelevant. The average *felláh* has fallen too low to be able to help himself without a great deal of compulsory assistance from the government. The system of government-controlled co-operatives in Egypt, moreover, did not originate with the Council of the Revolution. It originated with the Ministry of Social Affairs, which was established under the monarchy a generation ago. All that the republic has done is to extend the co-operative principle and apply it more rapidly than it was being applied under the monarchy.

Government intervention in the affairs of individuals can be an evil in some circumstances and a blessing in others. It can be a blessing in Egypt so long as it helps the *fellahín* to overcome the inertia resulting from the miserable existence they have led under previous regimes in which the government and the big landowners were one and the same thing. It can become an evil if the government coerces the peasants to the extent that they become the slaves of the state. We have no intention of exerting such coercion. Neither do we intend to intervene in the affairs of peasants who are capable of defending themselves. Hence the provision of the land reform decree whereby compulsory membership in co-operatives has been confined to peasants owning five acres or less. The moment a peasant acquires more than five acres he will be free to resign from his local co-operative if he so desires. Otherwise, like any other peasant, he may join the co-operative on a voluntary basis.

Nothing that we can do for the peasants, however, will achieve its purpose unless we can reclaim enough land to outpace the growth of Egypt's population. In order to do so, we must make more water available throughout the Nile Valley. This means that we must eventually build a high dam at Kalabsha, a few miles above the existing low dam at Asswan. Merely to increase the capacity of the existing dam and make better use of the water already available will not suffice. Unless the high dam is completed within a reasonable length of time our agrarian reforms will be defeated by the inevitable growth of our population.

The high dam, of course, cannot be built without foreign technical and financial assistance. Grateful as we have been for the technical assistance that we have been receiving from our American friends, the employees of TCA, such assistance will be unavailing in the long run unless we can count on the financial assistance necessary to dam up the Nile water now being wasted for lack of sufficient storage capacity in Upper Egypt. The high dam, which will cost approximately LE 180,000,000 ($516,600,000), will make it possible to increase Egypt's tillable acreage by from 30 to 60 per cent—that is, from the present 6,000,000 to a minimum of 8,000,000 and a maximum of 9,500,000 acres. It will also make it possible to industrialize Upper Egypt and supply the entire country with the cheap electricity that it so badly needs. If, in the meantime, with the help of TCA, we can learn to use our water more efficiently, there is a good chance, I think, of stabilizing the Egyptian economy at a relatively high standard of living within two generations.

VI

Ali Maher's failure to promulgate the land reform decree was but one of the reasons why it became necessary for me to succeed him as Prime Minister. Another reason, which was almost as important, was that he had failed to convince the Wafd and the other political parties that we meant what we said when we asked them to purge themselves of corruption. On September 10, I promulgated another decree law giving the parties one month in which to submit sworn statements to Suleiman Hafez, the then Minister of Interior, listing their objectives, officers, and the funds and properties at their disposal. The law authorized Hafez to prohibit any party whose objectives were not in the public interest or whose officers included anyone accused of corrupt practices or other crimes and misdemeanors.

The purpose of the law, as I explained at the time, was "to protect the people from political charlatanism." There was not a single party, including the Wafd, that represented anything but the personal interests and ambitions of its leaders. People who failed to understand the artificial nature of Egypt's parties were quick to criticize the Council of the Revolution for resorting to dictation. As events would prove, however, we were depriving only a few hundred corrupt politicians of the right to speak and act in the name of a people whom they had repeatedly betrayed.

Within a month no fewer than twenty-two parties, new and old, had duly registered with the Minister of Interior. All of them, I was amused to note, had listed identical objectives. There were five Moslem parties, including the Moslem Brothers, three feminist parties, including the Daughters of the Nile, two nationalist parties, two labor parties, and two Socialist parties, in addition to the Wafd and its three traditional rivals, the Sa'adist, the Liberal-Constitutional, and the *Kotla* (Fusion) parties. There was even a "Democratic Party," which, as might have been expected, turned out to be the Communist Party in disguise. None of the parties could offer a program that differed in any important respect from the program of the Council of the Revolution. Their only reason for existence was the conviction of their leaders that they were better able than we to do what none of them had ever seriously attempted to do before. But inasmuch as they had all fulfilled the letter, if not the spirit, of the political reform decree, we had no alternative but to let them function for the time being.

In the meantime the Council of the Revolution had arrested seventy-four persons accused of endangering the security of the state. Unfortunately, in trying to deal impartially with our enemies, my colleagues failed to separate the sheep from the goats. Thus, in addition to Pulli, Tabet, Serag ed Din, and others who deserved to be arrested, and were eventually tried and convicted, they also imprisoned Hilali and a number of other persons whose only offense was that they had held office under King Faruk. As soon as I could, I visited the prisoners at the Military Academy and assured them that the innocent among them would soon be released. Happily they were.

Because of such initial blunders a lot of people concluded that we didn't know what we were doing. We did. Our difficulty was that we didn't know how to do it. None of us had ever had any political experience, and, though my experience as a senior officer was helpful, it was not the sort of experience I needed to make the day-to-day decisions required of a Prime Minister. But little by little we learned our jobs, and eventually we assembled a fairly competent technical staff to assist us in our work.

In the beginning we had hoped to rely on certain elder states-
men and other men of experience in political, social, and economic
affairs to give us the advice and assistance that we so badly
needed. We soon discovered, however, that Egypt was sadly lacking in what the Americans call "dollar-a-year men"—the sort of
men who are able and willing to contribute their services to the
government in return for a dollar a year and nothing else but the
satisfaction of doing their patriotic duty in a time of crisis. There
were plenty of patriots in Egypt, but so few of them had been
given any encouragement in the past that they failed to rise to the
occasion. They were unable to understand that patriotism, to serve
its purpose, must rest on a highly developed sense of social responsibility. It is too much, I suppose, to expect to find much social
responsibility in any but countries that have long enjoyed responsible government. In a country like Egypt, which had been irre-
sponsibly governed for generations by the servants of a foreign
occupation, we were probably lucky to find as many responsible
collaborators as we did. But we need ten times as many as we
have, and we can only pray to God that our universities will produce them. Egyptians must mature politically as well as economically if we are ever to solve our problems.

VII

Our effort to clean up the political parties ended, as we feared
it would, in failure. Although the executive committee of the
Wafd expelled Serag ed Din and a number of other corruptionists, it refused to dismiss Nahass and attempted to trifle with the
law by making him its "honorary" president. While the left-wing
malcontents rallied to the cause of the "persecuted" Wafd, whose

leaders began to plot against us, the right-wing malcontents rallied round the person of the former head of the "persecuted" Sa'adist Party, Ibrahim Abd el Hadi. The Moslem Brothers, in the meantime, began to cry for Abd el Hadi's head. They accused him, as a former Prime Minister, of ordering the assassination of their founder and leader, Hassan el Banna, who in turn had been accused of ordering the assassination of Abd el Hadi's predecessor, Mahmúd Fahmi el Nokrashi.

In August there had been a bloody riot at the cotton mill of the Egyptian Spinning Company at Kafer el Dawar, a town not far from Alexandria. Inasmuch as the mill was a model factory in every way, with a free clinic, superb playing fields, and a cafeteria and commissary where meals, staple foods, and clothing were sold at less than cost, there was no discernible reason for the riot, which had obviously been inspired by enemies of the Revolution.

Twenty-nine persons were tried by a military tribunal on the factory grounds. As the trial progressed it became apparent that the persons responsible for the riot were members of the illegal Communist Party, which is known in Egypt as "Haditu" because of its Arabic initials. A few days earlier the same Communists had inspired a strike in the plant of the Beida Dyeing Company, which is also located at Kafer el Dawar. Beida's managers had recognized the newly organized union and granted an increase in wages. When the Communists attempted to organize a strike at the Egyptian Company's cotton mill, however, its managers called the police. Four persons were arrested. Two days later, as the night shift was going on duty, a group of agitators began to demand the immediate dismissal of the personnel manager and several other company officials. As soon as they had drawn a crowd they set fire to some hayricks, which they had stationed in the parking lot, and which they used in turn to set fire to a score of automobiles and trucks before they stormed the company offices. Policemen and soldiers had to be called in to restore order. The result was that nine persons, including a policeman and two soldiers, were killed, and twenty-three persons, including seven policemen, were seriously wounded.

We decided that the only way to deal with the situation was to make an example of those who had started the riot. The principal culprit was a young man named Mustafa Khamís. He and a guard named Mohammed Hassan el Bákhari were convicted of high treason and sentenced to death. Twelve others were sentenced to prison terms ranging from five to fifteen years and fifteen others were acquitted. Inasmuch as Khamís was only twenty-one years old, I was eager to give him another chance. I accordingly invited him to come to Cairo to see me in my office. Like Bákhari, he had entered a plea of not guilty, but had refused to co-operate with the prosecution. He had clearly been ordered to start the riot by persons who have yet to be identified and who were willing to let him die in order to save themselves. I offered to commute his sentence to life imprisonment, which in Egypt means twenty-five years with time off for good behavior, if he would but name the persons who had given him his orders. But Khamís refused, and so I had no alternative but to approve his sentence. On September 8, the day after I succeeded Maher as Prime Minister, he and Bákhari were hanged.

Two days later a different sort of riot occurred in the village of Maghagha, near Minia, in Upper Egypt. A wealthy young landowner named Adli Lamlúm galloped into Maghagha at the head of a band of thirty-five armed horsemen. After firing shots into the air in cowboy fashion, they rounded up the villagers, to whom Lamlúm delivered the following ultimatum: There would be no land reform in Maghagha so long as the Lamlúms were running things; any peasants attempting to profit from their expropriation would be killed. (The Lamlúm family owned approximately 2000 acres, from which they derived an annual income of LE 180,000 or $536,000.)

The next day, after local officials had promised the peasants that they would be allowed to purchase the Lamlúms' surplus acreage, in spite of Adli's threats, he and his men returned to Maghagha to repeat the performance of the day before. This time they were confronted by some soldiers and policemen, who ordered them to disperse. A few shots were exchanged and a policeman and a woman onlooker were wounded. Lamlúm and four of his men were arrested; the others fled.

We decided to proceed in the Maghagha affair exactly as we had proceeded at Kafer el Dawar. Lamlúm and eight of his men were tried before a military tribunal in Minia. On October 8, since no one had been killed in his little riot, Lamlúm, who was then twenty-four, was sentenced to life imprisonment. Five of his followers received prison sentences ranging from five to fifteen years; three were acquitted.

VIII

Thanks to our firm handling of these and a number of other incidents, it was a long time before any more civilians resorted to armed rebellion. Inside the Army, though, a number of malcontents began to conspire with Mohammed Rashad Mehanna to overthrow the government. Mehanna, in his capacity as regent, had been attempting to formulate a policy of his own in direct opposition to that of the Council of the Revolution. Early in

October, after he had failed to heed our repeated warnings, we dismissed him from the Council of Regents and placed him under house arrest. Bahi ed Din Barakát, who was also jealous of his prerogatives, resigned in protest, and on October 14 I appointed Prince Abd el Moneim the sole Regent of Egypt. Abd el Moneim, who understood our position as well as his own, co-operated loyally until we abolished the regency and founded the republic, at which time he retired from public life.

A few days after his dismissal and arrest, I went to call on Mehanna at his home. He apologized so profusely for all the trouble he had caused us that I persuaded my colleagues to set him free. No sooner had he been freed, however, than he began to behave as he had done before. He criticized the land reform, which he denounced as a "Communist maneuver," and accused the Council of the Revolution of attempting to destroy Islam in Egypt by establishing a "godless" republic.

In a radio address on December 10, I announced the abrogation of the Constitution of 1923.

"When the Army began the Revolution on 23 July," I recalled, "the country was in a state of corruption and deterioration as the result of the misrule of a profligate King, abominable standards of political behavior, and an unsound system of parliamentary government. . . .

"The King used the Constitution as a means of justifying his behavior. With the help of those who governed the country in his name, he discovered loopholes in the Constitution that made it possible for him to violate its principles.

"This is why we began the Revolution. Its object was not only to get rid of the King but . . . to establish a healthy political life based on liberty, justice, and discipline, to the end that the Egyptian people might devote their energies to productive work in the interests of the country.

"Now that the work of reconstruction has begun—and it embraces all fields of human endeavor, political, social, and economic—the time has come to change those institutions which have almost ruined the country and which are based on loopholes in the old Constitution. . . .

"In the name of the people, therefore, I hereby abrogate the Constitution of 1923. . . . [The] government is now forming a committee to draw up a new Constitution, to be approved by the people, that will be free of the defects of the old. The new Constitution will be so drafted as to realize the people's desire for clean and sound parliamentary government.

"During the inevitable period of transition, and pending the approval of the new Constitution, the present government will assume full powers. It also assumes before God and country the obligation of protecting the interests of all citizens without discrimination and with due regard for established constitutional principles. . . ."

Anwar es Sadát had meanwhile explained in a press conference that the new Constitution would be submitted to the people in the course of a referendum in which they would also be asked to decide whether Egypt should be a monarchy or a republic.

Although we were thus preparing the ground for the establishment of a secular republic, we had no intention, as Mehanna well knew, of dispensing with religion. Islam would continue to be the official religion of Egypt, yet the freedom of all religious faiths would continue to be guaranteed. The religious clauses of the new Constitution would be identical to those of the old.

Mehanna, however, chose to conspire against us on the ground that a secular republic would be inimical to Islam. We waited until he had completed his preparations for a counterrevolution and then, on January 17, we arrested him and his fellow conspirators. At the same time, to demonstrate our impartiality, we arrested a number of Communist conspirators and suspended six Communist newspapers. We also arrested the governor of the Western Desert, Lieutenant Colonel Mohammed Husni el Damanhuri, who, with the knowledge of his brother, Captain Hassan Rifa'at el Damanhuri, had been plotting a countercoup of his own.

On January 20 the Damanhuris were tried before a military tribunal. Mohammed was sentenced to death and Hassan to five years in prison. I later commuted Mohammed's sentence to life imprisonment and suspended Hassan's sentence after discharging him from the Army.

On March 30, after being tried in camera by the entire Council of the Revolution, Mehanna was sentenced to life imprisonment. Thirteen of his fellow conspirators received prison sentences ranging from one to fifteen years.

Thus ended the first phase of the Egyptian Revolution and the regrettable purge that was necessary to ensure the accomplishment of its objectives.

5

THE REPUBLIC

On January 23, 1953, we began a four-day celebration of our first six months in power. Inasmuch as the celebration overlapped the anniversary of the burning of Cairo, on January 26, 1952, we took advantage of the occasion to emphasize our efforts to do away with the conditions that had produced the incendiary riots. We also took advantage of the occasion to abolish all of Egypt's political parties except the Moslem Brotherhood. Although I doubted the wisdom of excepting the Moslem Brothers, I supported my junior colleagues' decision to replace the other parties with a single united front. The purpose of the united front, which we called the Liberation Rally, was to prepare the people to participate on a national scale in the new political parties that we hoped to create before the third anniversary of the Revolution. During the intervening three-year period of transition, the Council of the Revolution would rule Egypt by decree in the interests of national reconstruction. A five-year plan, which was later to become a ten-year plan, was inaugurated at the same time. It was our original hope to achieve our major objectives within five years. We soon discovered, however, that we had been too optimistic, and so we revised our program of political, social, and economic development to conform to a slower rate of progress.

Many foreigners as well as Egyptians have criticized our abolition of political parties as an authoritarian maneuver designed to perpetuate the dictatorship of the Council of the Revolution. Such criticism has usually been based on the mistaken assumption that the parties we abolished were genuine expressions of diverse trends in Egyptian public opinion. Unfortunately they were not. They were merely expressions of the political ambitions of their leaders.

Even the Wafd, which was by far the strongest of the old parties, represented only those individuals who hoped to exploit Mustafa en Nahass as Sa'ad Zaghlul's successor. Whatever Nahass may have represented in his younger days—and there was a time when he was a truly popular leader—he surrounded himself in his old age with some of the most unwholesome figures in Egyptian public life. Had he renounced his hangers-on and espoused the cause of the Revolution, he might have been able to restore the Wafd to the status of a genuine party. Instead he chose to allow the parasites who surrounded him to make common cause with the Communists and the Moslem Brothers in the hope of undermining the Revolution and restoring the sort of conditions that had prevailed when the Wafd was last in power.

Many Wafdists believe that even today they could win a "free" election—by which they mean the sort of "free" elections that have been held in Egypt in the past. But how "free" is an election in which the party with the most money can bribe village officials to produce unanimous votes in its favor? How "free" is an election in which the majority of candidates are not even residents of the districts that they presume to represent? And, finally, how "free" is an election in which the majority of voters are illiterate peasants who vote the way they are told to vote for fear of reprisals if they do not?

No, I am sorry to say, there has never been a really free election in Egypt, nor can there be until the political structure of every village, town, and city has been changed. Voters must be free to know the qualifications and programs of the various candidates for public office. Each candidate must be a bona fide resident of the district that he is supposed to represent. Government officials and others must be prevented from buying or influencing votes. And the victorious party must be prevented from creating its own dictatorship as soon as it comes to power.

Next to the Wafd, the most powerful political organization in Egypt before the Revolution was the Moslem Brotherhood. Although the Moslem Brothers had never taken part in an election, they exercised a disproportionate influence on Egyption policy by inflaming the religious emotions of the man in the street. Since they refused to admit that they were a political party, even though they had registered as one, it was decided not to abolish them for the time being but to attempt to fuse them with the Liberation Rally. In the end we had to arrest a lot of their leaders in order to purge the Rally of their subversive influence. But we waited so long to do so, unfortunately, that they were able to assume the role of a "persecuted minority." We would have done better, I think, to abolish the Moslem Brotherhood along with all the other parties in the early days of the Revolution. Had we done so, the Liberation Rally would have gathered strength more rapidly than it has, and we would be nearer than we are today to the creation of a new system of popular suffrage adapted to the realities of Egyptian life.

The Liberation Rally, which amounts to a temporary one-party system, has pledged its members to support the following program:

1. Complete and unconditional withdrawal of foreign troops from the Nile Valley.

2. Self-determination for Sudan.

3. A new Constitution expressing the fundamental aspirations of the Egyptian people.

4. A social system in which all citizens shall be entitled to protection against the ravages of unemployment, illness, and old age —i.e., a "welfare state."

5. An economic system designed to encourage a fair distribution of wealth, full exploitation of natural and human resources, and the maximum investment of new capital.

6. A political system in which all citizens shall be equal before the law and in which freedom of speech, assembly, press, and religion shall be guaranteed within the limits of the law.

7. An educational system designed to develop a sense of social responsibility by impressing youth with its duties as well as its rights and with the overriding need to increase production in order to raise Egypt's standard of living.

8. Friendly relations with all Arab states.

9. A regional pact designed to increase the influence of the Arab League.

10. Friendly relations with all friendly powers.

11. Firm adherence to the principles of the United Nations, with special emphasis on their application to subject peoples.

After reviewing a civilian and military parade, and delivering a speech to the multitude assembled in the Midán el Ismailía, the largest square in Cairo, which was henceforth to be called the Midán el Hurría (Freedom Square), I asked the crowd to repeat after me the following prayer:

"Almighty God, You love the strong and despise the weak. You spread Your mercy over those who prefer to die for their liberty rather than to live in a state of servitude.

"Almighty God, You are close to us and can hear our prayer. We swear by Your Holy Name to do our utmost to lay the foundations of a future life in which our beloved country shall be freed from bondage and from all evil passions and devoted to all that is just and right. To this end we will make every sacrifice required by the interests and honor of our country, and our motto at all times will be: Unity, Discipline, and Work.

"Almighty God, the Best of Witnesses, be our witness on this day."

A liberation flag, consisting of red, white, and black horizontal bars (signifying the new blood of the future, the purity of our ideals, and the black corruption of the past), was unfurled for the occasion, and a liberation hymn, which had already been widely sung, was adopted as the anthem of the revolutionary movement. (A new national anthem to replace that of the monarchy has yet to be selected; for the time being we are still using a modified version of the old.)

Three weeks later I promulgated a provisional Constitution by virtue of which the Council of the Revolution would govern Egypt for the remainder of the period of transition. The provisional Constitution consists of the following articles:

I. The people are the source of all authority.

II. All Egyptians are equal before the law as regards their rights and obligations.

III. Freedom of person and freedom of thought shall be guaranteed within the limits of the law. An Egyptian's home and property shall be inviolable within the limits of the law.

IV. Freedom of conscience shall be guaranteed, and the state shall protect the practice of religious rites in accordance with established usage, provided such rites are compatible with morality and do not disturb the maintenance of public order.

V. The extradition of political refugees is prohibited.

VI. No tax may be imposed except by law, nor may any fee be imposed except by law, nor may anyone be exempted from the payment of any tax or fee except as provided by law.

VII. The judiciary is independent and subject only to the law. Its judgments are to be pronounced and executed in the name of the people.

VIII. The Leader of the Revolution, on behalf of the Council of the Revolution, shall assume full sovereign powers, particularly in regard to measures deemed necessary to protect the Revolution and the . . . attainment of its objectives, as well as the right to appoint and dismiss ministers.

IX. The Council of Ministers [cabinet] shall exercise the legislative power.

X. The Council of Ministers and each individual minister shall exercise the executive power in so far as it has been delegated.

XI. The Council of the Revolution and the Council of Ministers shall meet jointly to consider the general policy of the state and . . . to supervise the work of individual ministers.

In assuming full powers on the basis of the provisional Constitution, I promised the Egyptian people that I would restore a "democratic, constitutional regime at the end of the [three-year] period of transition [in order to ensure] the bright future of the free and dignified life for which all of us are working."

II

I thus became a "reluctant dictator," as I was called in the foreign press, in spite of the fact that, in one of my first interviews with a foreign correspondent, I had said that I would not become a dictator of any sort "if I could possibly avoid it."

Could I have avoided the assumption of dictatorial powers on February 10, 1953?

Looking back on what has happened since, I honestly do not think I could. The Egyptian Revolution, though it was passively supported by the great majority, was actively supported by only a small minority of the people. Its enemies, who were also only a small minority, were nevertheless sufficiently strong to have destroyed the Revolution had we not taken stern measures to prevent them from doing so.

In becoming a dictator, albeit reluctantly, I exposed myself to the criticism of those who wanted me to be more of a dictator than I was capable of being as well as of those who did not want me to be a dictator at all. Ever since the revolution in Turkey, people had been talking of the supposed need for an "Egyptian Atatürk," and for a time it was thought by some that even Faruk could play the role. After the Revolution in Egypt it was I who was expected to become the "Egyptian Atatürk," and, when I declined to play the role, it was thought that Abd el Nasser would take it up. I do not think, however, that even he can be said to have become an "Egyptian Atatürk," though he has succeeded me as the Prime Minister.

The Egyptians and the Turks are two very different peoples. Whereas the Turks have never lost their independence, we Egyptians have never fully recovered ours since we were conquered by the Persians in 525 B.C. After having been Iranized, Hellenized, Romanized, and Byzantinized, we were Arabized in the seventh century only to be Ottomanized in the thirteenth. Six centuries later we were Gallicized by Napoleon and Anglicized by a succession of British proconsuls, including Cromer, Kitchener, and Allenby. Today we are at last in a position to reclaim the national sovereignty of which we have so long been deprived. But if we are to assert it successfully we must conform to cosmopolitan standards of behavior. Otherwise we may find ourselves in an unequal conflict with the world powers whose strategic interests are involved in the Suez Canal.

Turkey occupies a similar position athwart the Bosphorus and the Dardanelles. But, for all their importance to Russia and the Western Powers, the Straits are far less important than the Canal as an artery of trade and communications. Whereas Turkey is a relatively homogeneous and self-sufficient country, occupying the rich peninsula of Asia Minor, Egypt is but a chain of oases surrounded by deserts and inhabited not only by Egyptians but by large and influential minorities of varying cultural backgrounds. It was hard enough for Atatürk to do what he did in Turkey, and the country, for all its advances, has yet to recover from the shock of his ruthless personality. It would be ruinous, in my opinion, for Egyptians to attempt to emulate the experience of the Turks. We could never survive the isolation to which the Turks, like the Russians (though on a much smaller scale), were subjected in the midst of their revolution. Just as Greece is an archipelago in a sea of water, so Egypt is an archipelago in a sea of sand. Both countries must engage in trade in order to survive.

Even Turkey has found it necessary to admit foreign capital in order to accelerate its industrialization. Egypt's foreign capital requirements are proportionately greater than Turkey's. They are so great, in fact, that it will be impossible, without foreign capital, for us to industrialize quickly enough to arrest our declining standard of living. Foreign capital, I have observed, is not attracted to countries whose economies are rigidly controlled. Prosperity depends, in the last analysis, on free trade, and free trade flourishes in inverse proportion to governmental interference.

Another reason why the Egyptian Revolution has not produced an Atatürk is that it has been led from the very beginning by a committee rather than an individual. The decisions of the Council of the Revolution depend on the will of the majority of its members. The rule of a committee, for obvious reasons, can never be as efficient as the rule of an individual. But there are strengths as well as weaknesses in committee rule. Even though its authority is divided and its decisions are the results of compromise, a committee is likely to be more responsive than an individual to the ebb and flow of public opinion. The dictatorship that I originally headed and which is now headed by Abd el Nasser has thus been less oppressive than a personal dictatorship might have been— and the extirpation of oppression has always been one of the objectives of the Egyptian Revolution.

Our relations with Sudan and the other Arab states were also responsible for my decision not to become an "Egyptian Atatürk." In the beginning, it will be recalled, we were accused of acting under the inspiration of Communists, Fascists, and Moslem Brothers. In order to demonstrate the falsity of these accusations it was necessary to avoid behaving like Fascists, Communists, and Moslem Brothers; and in order to win the sympathy of the Sudanese, with whom we desire the closest of friendly relations, it was necessary to demonstrate that we had nothing in common with the oppressive regimes that had misruled the Nile Valley in

the past. The Sudanese were ready to co-operate with us in ex-
pelling the British from our common valley, but they had no
desire to exchange British for Egyptian masters. We had to convince them, as well as some of our other Arab neighbors, that
the aggrandizement of Egypt at their expense was no part of our
revolutionary program.

But the most important reason why I declined to become an
Atatürk is the character of the Egyptian people themselves. Unlike the Turks, the Egyptians are not inclined to accept authoritarian rule as a matter of course; on the contrary, we are inclined
to resent authoritarianism unless it can be shown to be in our
own best interests. Thus, although a mild dictatorship was necessary for the attainment of our objectives, I did my best to make
it a persuasive rather than a coercive dictatorship. Egyptians will
follow anyone who sets the right example; by the same token, they
will turn on anyone who violates their principles, which are a
product of their traditions, or who attempts to impose new principles by force alone. I therefore made myself as accessible to the
people as I possibly could. I felt that if I could convince them
that I was one of them I could persuade them to do a lot of things
that they could never be forced to do. Against the advice of the
men whose job it was to protect my life, I violated the principles
of security in order to test my principles of leadership. I traveled
throughout the country listening patiently to everyone's com-
plaints. I encouraged people to petition the government to redress
their grievances, and I personally saw to it that thousands of
grievances were redressed. I spoke to the people in their own
language, and in my speeches, most of which were extemporane-
ous, I confined myself to the use of simple phrases and expressions
that they could understand. That no attempt has yet been made
on my life is proof, I think, that my approach to the Egyptian
people was correct.

Only once, to my knowledge, has anyone even threatened to do me violence. As I was driving home from my office one day in July 1953, I noticed a ragged old man shaking his fist at me and shouting, "*Ya zalem, ya zalem* [Oh, tyrant, oh, tyrant]!" He was too old to do me any harm, but I could tell from the expression on his face that he would have tried to do so had he been given the opportunity. I stopped my car and told the captain of the guard who was following me in a jeep to bring the old man to see me at my home. He turned out to be a burglar and safecracker named Ahmed Mohammed Mansúr. He had been arrested thirty-three times, he said, and had spent a total of twenty-eight years in various prisons. Although he wanted to earn an honest living, the police had refused to let him do so. His application for a license to sell soft drinks had been rejected because of his criminal record. I gave a five-pound note to the captain of the guard and told him to buy Mohammed an ice chest and a few cases of drinks. The officers of the guard, as I later learned, added another five pounds to my contribution and bought him some new clothes. The old man has been happily, honestly, and, technically speaking, illegally employed ever since—at the entrance to one of our police stations.

Mohammed is but one of hundreds of unfortunates whom I have gone out of my way to help. I mention him only to illustrate my conviction that the Egyptian people can be more easily led by kindly gestures than by threats. On July 23, 1954, in honor of the second anniversary of the Revolution, we freed some 600 convicts who had satisfied the authorities that they were able and willing to reform. They were paroled in the care of employers who had volunteered to give them jobs and see to it that they resisted temptation in the future. Ever since I was a colonel, when a servant whom I had dismissed revealed to me that he was un-

able to obtain another job because he had once been arrested
for vagrancy, I have been trying to revise the Egyptian penal
code. It is much too hard on petty offenders, in my opinion,
many of whom have been driven to a life of crime because of
their inability to earn an honest living.

The help I gave to old Mohammed and the others was less
a matter of charity than of practical politics. (I have adopted
an orphaned baby girl for the same reason.) I consider it my
duty to demonstrate that justice in all its forms is the essence
of the Egyptian Revolution, and I can think of no better way
of doing so than by setting frequent examples for my fellow countrymen to follow. Nor have I been alone in this endeavor. The
Council of the Revolution sponsored a winter relief campaign
that was so successful in 1952–53 that it was repeated with even
greater success under the auspices of the Liberation Rally in
1953–54. Winter relief has now become an Egyptian institution.
Charity had previously been a matter of the individual conscience;
now, thanks to the Revolution, it is becoming a matter of the col-
lective social conscience, which we have done everything in our
power to encourage. It is not poverty itself, I have found, that
breeds Communists and other extremists; it is rather the indifference of the well to do to the misery of the poor.

III

Social justice, important though it is, will not suffice to solve
Egypt's problems in the absence of spiritual brotherhood. One
of the greatest achievements of Sa'ad Zaghlul was that he made
it possible for Moslems and Copts to work together for the good
of Egypt regardless of their differences. Someday, if the ideals

of the Revolution prevail, it will be possible for the Greeks, Jews, Armenians, Syrians, Lebanese, and other minorities to follow in the footsteps of the Copts.[1]

The greatest fault of the Moslem Brothers, in my opinion, is that by emphasizing and exaggerating the differences between the Moslem majority and the Christian and Jewish minorities they have aroused misgivings in the minds of the minorities as to their future relations with Egyptian Moslems. Both as Prime Minister and as President, therefore, I have had to go to great lengths to persuade the minorities that the new Egypt will be as tolerant as any state in the world.

Anyone who takes the trouble to study the history of the Islamic peoples will find, I think, that they have been less intolerant, on the whole, than many of the Christian peoples. Nationalism, I know, has often bred intolerance in the past. In an age when atomic weapons ought to have made internationalists of us all, however, I do not feel that any country can afford to indulge in xenophobia. Independence, far from exacerbating xenophobia in Egypt, will actually reduce it, I believe, for most of the anti-foreign outbreaks that have occurred in recent years have been due to two factors that are now beginning to disappear. The first is the frustration resulting from Great Britain's refusal to keep its repeated promises to evacuate the Suez Canal Zone. The second is the jealousy aroused by the privileged position enjoyed in the past by those members of the various minorities who have co-operated with the British in prolonging a hated occupation.

[1]The Copts, who today number approximately 1,500,000, are descendants of the Monophysite Christian majority in Egypt at the time of the Arab invasion. Egyptian Moslems, who today number approximately 20,000,000, are mostly descendants of Coptic converts to Islam. The word "Copt," like the word "Egypt," is a corruption of the original word (*"Ha-ke-Ptah"*) for an inhabitant of Egypt.

Now that evacuation has at last begun, and the occupation is coming to a belated end, there can be no question of any more special privileges. From now on all Egyptians will be equal before the law. And by "equal" I mean exactly what I say. Just as no special privileges will be extended to any minority, neither will any special privileges be extended to the Moslem majority. The day of special privileges in Egypt is over. Rich and poor; black, brown, and white; Moslem, Christian, and Jew—we shall all be Egyptians together in what I hope will be the modern equivalent of the cosmopolitan society that flourished under the Umayad Dynasty in Spain.

In order to convince the minorities that the Revolution is devoid of religious prejudices, I have attended Christian and Jewish religious services of every important rite. The first non-Moslem religious service that I attended, in fact, was the celebration of *Yom Kippúr* (The Day of Atonement) in the Ismailía synagogue in Cairo. Later I lead the prayers at the Karaite synagogue in Abbassía. I have also attended Coptic services, Greek and Armenian Orthodox services, Catholic services, Maronite services, and Protestant services.

On one of the walls of my house, along with several quotations from the Koran, I have hung a picture that was presented to me by a Coptic priest. It represents the hand of God patting my heart. I have also worn a medal of St. Christopher from time to time. The medal was sent to me by a Greek woman who wrote that God had appeared to her in a dream and commanded her to ask me to wear it. I have done so, even though I am a Moslem, for I believe that the same God is the Creator of us all and that it is less important how we worship Him than that we should worship Him sincerely.

One of the Islamic institutions that most appeals to me is the annual pilgrimage. In Mecca and Medina, in the heart of Arabia, worshipers from all over the world gather under a pitiless sun to do homage to the one God Who could unite us all if we were but willing to be united. I have gone on two pilgrimages so far, in 1950 and again in 1953, and I hope to go on several more before I die. In 1950, I went alone to Mecca and Medina to thank God for having saved my life, to pray for my daughter, even though I knew that her disease was fatal, and to implore God to let mine be the hand that would overthrow King Faruk. In 1953 my wife and eldest son Faruk were also pilgrims, though we traveled separately. In that year, as I pondered the life of the Prophet, I implored the Almighty to save me from the intoxication of pride and to fill me with respect for the rights of others. I vowed to face God on Judgment Day without having to account for a single rightful demand that I had failed to grant, a single act of injustice for which I had not atoned, or a single appeal for help that I had left unanswered. As I stood before the tomb of the Prophet, I thought of the past glories of the Islamic peoples and compared them with our situation in the world today.

"Why," I asked myself, "are we treated with such scant consideration that we have become the target of the ambitious, the powerful, and those who claim to be so?"

An answer soon occurred to me: The evil that has befallen us is due to our indifference to the fate of those who live among us. We have treated our fellow men with contempt instead of respect, and we have disregarded the rights of others.

While visiting the tombs of Abu Bahker el Saddík and Omar el Faruk, the first and second *khalifas* (caliphs), I thought of the struggle that they had had to wage, of how the former had won the hearts of the would-be renegades, and of how the latter had so successfully administered justice in his time that he was able to sleep by the roadside without fear of attack from any quarter. In these holy places I prayed to God to make it possible for Egyptians to enjoy the same faith and the same security and to recover the dignity, generosity, and spirit of self-sacrifice that Islam had given to our ancestors. Today, as I write these lines, on the second anniversary of the Egyptian Revolution, I have the feeling that my prayer is being answered.

The renewal of faith in the brotherhood of man—such is the meaning of the pilgrimage, and such, I fancy, is the meaning of the great rites of all the great religions. It behooves none of us in this time of troubles, when all of us are menaced by the same enemies of God, to carp at the faith of others. On the contrary, it behooves us all to renew our own faith, whatever it may be, and to make use of that faith to defend our common civilization by improving the condition of our fellow men.

IV

On June 18, 1953, the world's oldest kingdom became, for the time being, the world's youngest republic. In becoming its President as well as its Prime Minister, I was succeeded as Commander in Chief of the Armed Forces by my youthful colleague Abd el Hakím Amer, who was exceptionally promoted from the rank of major to that of major general. Abd el Latíf Baghdadi succeeded me as Minister of War. Abd el Nasser, who succeeded Suleiman Hafez as Minister of Interior, became my Vice-Prime Minister. Saláh Salem succeeded Fuad Galál as Minister of National Guidance (Propaganda) and also assumed the new post of Minister of State for Sudanese Affairs. Titles were abolished, as was the regency headed by Prince Abd el Moneim, and the infant Ahmed Fuad II was officially deposed.

The decision to proclaim Egypt a republic before the new Constitution had been submitted to the people was not taken lightly. Although my junior colleagues would have preferred to proclaim the republic even earlier, they had refrained from doing so on the advice of myself and others who believed that the people should be given an opportunity to vote on the question of monarchy versus republic at the same time as they were consulted regarding the Constitution. We had counted on the regency to provide us with the necessary stability to hold the promised referendum. Unfortunately, through no fault of Abd el Moneim, the regency failed to serve its purpose. Far from being a stabilizing influence, its very existence encouraged our enemies, right and left, to plot against us. We therefore proclaimed the republic by decree in order to put an end to the institutional uncertainties on which our enemies were thriving.

The decision to militarize the cabinet by making ministers of four additional members of the Council of the Revolution was of doubtful wisdom, in my opinion. Inasmuch as I was to be both President and Prime Minister, however, it would have been out of place for me to oppose my colleagues' desire to assume open control of certain ministries. I think it would have been better, even so, had we continued to allow civilians to head the civilian ministries under the discreet guidance of the Council of the Revolution. We could have thus avoided the accusation of our enemies that we were as interested in holding public office as we were in achieving the objectives of the Revolution. The accusation gained particular currency after Gamál Salem became the Minister of Communications and Zakaria Mohi ed Din the Minister of Interior. The militarization of the government, in fact, was one of the reasons why I resigned as Prime Minister in February 1954.

We had been paying Regent Abd el Moneim (and his two colleagues, before they resigned) a salary of LE 9000 ($25,830) a year. It was at first suggested that I be paid the same salary while forgoing my salary as Prime Minister. Later, in view of the austerity program that we had decided to adopt, it was suggested that I be paid LE 6000 ($17,220). In the end, as an example to my fellow countrymen, I agreed to forgo half this lesser salary and to accept only LE 3000 ($8610). It was the least I could do, I felt, at a time when we were asking all government employees to accept temporary reductions in their income.[2]

The question then arose as to whether I should move with my family into Abdín Palace (now called the Palace of the Republic) or whether I should continue to reside in my rented bungalow in Helmíet el Zeitún. There were a number of practical arguments in favor of moving into the palace, but in the end I decided to go on living in my bungalow in spite of all its disadvantages. It was a long way from the center of Cairo and it lacked most of the amenities normally associated with the residence of a chief of state. Yet its very modesty was a psychological argument in its favor. Had I moved into the palace, I would have felt like a hypocrite in urging my fellow countrymen to observe our program of austerity. So long as I continued to live in a simple manner, however, I would be justified in urging those of my countrymen who could afford to do so to sacrifice their luxuries in the interests of national reconstruction. Besides, as I remarked to a group of journalists after swearing in my new

---

[2]After paying my income tax on the basis of a real income of LE 3000, and my pension contributions on the basis of a theoretical income of LE 6000, I have been earning less as President than I was earning as Prime Minister.

cabinet, I liked my little house and felt that, thus far, it had brought me luck.

On June 23, eleven months after the coup d'état, I was sworn in as the President of Egypt in the presence of my ministers and the other members of the Council of the Revolution. The ceremony was performed on the balcony of the Republican Palace in the presence of a crowd that completely filled the square below us. As soon as I had taken my oath, Abd el Nasser, speaking over a microphone, asked the crowd to repeat after him the following prayer:

"Almighty and Omniscient God, be our witness to the fact that we have invested General Mohammed Naguib, the Leader of the Revolution, as the President of Egypt. We swear to protect the republic with all our strength and determination and to work for the liberation of our country with all our heart and soul. We swear that our slogan will always be: Unity, Discipline, and Work. . . ."

Shaikh Mohammed el Kader Hussein, the then rector of the Moslem university, El Azhar, delivered the first of the speeches that preceded my inaugural address. Shaikh Mohammed was followed by Patriarch Yussab II, who spoke on behalf of the Copts and other Christians, and by Haim Nahúm, the Grand Rabbi, who, because he was ill, allowed his speech to be read for him on behalf of the Jews. A student spoke in the name of Egyptian youth, and a workman in the name of Egyptian labor. I then delivered my own speech, in the course of which, among other things, I said:

". . . Thanks to the Revolution, we have won the confidence of the entire world. . . . With self-control, patience, and caution, while doing our utmost to increase such confidence, we can reap the best and greatest of fruits—independence.

"Egypt in the past was governed on the basis of favoritism and bribery. Government was a matter of improvisation. We have begun a relentless war against this type of government, a war of life and death for every citizen. Let everyone draw his sword and strike at the evils of the past. Let no one say that the extirpation of bribery, favoritism, and parasitism are the responsibility of the government alone. When an epidemic breaks out, it does no good to fight it unless the authorities can count on the co-operation of every individual citizen. Let us seek out those who give and take bribes and see that they receive the punishment they deserve. . . . Let us stand up for our rights and see that government officials serve the interests of the people. Let us teach them that they are our servants, not our masters, and that a good servant is both prompt and energetic. Let us be the eyes of the state so that every abuse may be corrected. Let us forget our cynical attitudes of the past, for cynicism is but a confession of helplessness in the face of evil. . . .

"Let the family spirit prevail among us so that no one may say that such and such a task is no concern of his. Let us remember that there is no place in Egypt today for spectators. Egypt is badly in need of the effort of every individual, the enthusiasm of every heart, the intelligence of every brain. . . . Once we learn the meaning of unity and discipline, our lives will be secure, and there will be no problem too difficult for us to solve.

"Our enemies will then disperse, for their only hope is that dissension will spread among us. They are acting on the assumption that, like our predecessors, we are not seriously interested in attaining our objectives, that we are dealing in words rather than deeds. . . . They are acting on the assumption that poverty, ignorance, and disease will continue to plague us in spite of all we say and do. They believe that we are afraid. Let us prove them wrong by acting in accordance with Koranic teachings:

" 'And these to whom the people said, "Others are plotting against you, beware," were only strengthened in their faith, and said, "It is sufficient to have God as our champion." And by the grace of God they were not harmed. Seek God's approval, for in Him there is much grace. . . .'

"My compatriots: In a similar situation, Abu Bahker el Saddík addressed the believers, saying, 'O people, I have been proclaimed your ruler even though I am not the best among you. If you approve of my conduct, help me, but, if you disapprove of my conduct, correct me.'

"I cannot find better words with which to close than those uttered by the pure heart of El Saddík. I appeal to you to be vigilant so that righteousness may be my watchword and the cornerstone of my government; to help me as long as it is, and to correct me whenever it is not. . . ."

V

The Egyptian republic, despite all the dire predictions to the contrary, has proved to be a success. We have made mistakes and we have quarreled among ourselves. At one time we were on the verge of civil war. But, thanks to God, the Beneficent, the Merciful, the republic has survived its tribulations; and though individuals may have suffered—some of them, I fear, unjustly—the people as a whole have gained a great deal that they could have gained in no other way.

We have had to pay for our Revolution, as we must pay for everything in life, but I see no reason to believe that the price so far has been too high. I had hoped that it would be possible to consolidate the republic without any further purges. But, alas, in spite of my pleas, the people were not sufficiently vigilant to prevent their enemies from continuing to plot against them. By September 13, eight months after the founding of the Liberation Rally, dissension had become so rife that we found it necessary to organize yet another celebration, in the course of which we restated the purposes of the Revolution in the sharpest possible terms.

In an effort to encourage voluntary co-operation, we had abolished censorship in all its forms. Instead of respecting the gesture, our enemies took advantage of it to smuggle currency out of the country through the mails and to publish rumors designed to undermine the security of the state. The press, instead of using its freedom to enlighten the public, indulged in an orgy of misinformation. There was nothing to do but restore censorship for the duration of the transitional period. We knew that in so doing we would be criticized abroad. We hoped, however, that the foreign correspondents in Egypt, who have not been censored since the Revolution, would continue to report the news in such a way that our friends abroad would be able to appreciate our predicament. And, with few exceptions, the free press of the Western world has been faithful to its trust.

I wish I could say as much for the Egyptian press, but unfortunately I cannot. Its representatives, with few exceptions, have yet to learn that there can be no freedom in the absence of responsibility. The Council of the Revolution had no objection to criticism, provided it was based on facts and inspired by a genuine desire to correct abuses. What we could not tolerate, and what no government in any country could tolerate for very long, was the publication, day after day, of unfounded rumors. The Egyptian press is a youthful press, but its relative youth is no excuse for its continued irresponsibility. The time has come for Egyptian publishers, editors, and reporters to adopt and enforce a code of ethics. On the day they prove that they can be trusted as a group to seek, find, and print the truth—or at least a reasonable approximation of the truth—it will be possible to dispense with censorship. But not, I fear, until then.

It was not only with "the cockroaches who spread rumors," as I called them, with whom we had to deal; we also had to deal with an increasing number of spies and traitors in the pay of various foreign powers. If I refrain from naming the powers concerned, it is not because there is any lack of evidence of their illegal intervention in our internal affairs. It is only because we cannot afford, in the midst of a Revolution, to become embroiled in quarrels with foreign states. The evidence exists, but its nature is such that it would serve no useful purpose for me to mention any details here.

Our solution to the problem of subversion was to emulate the French. We created a Tribunal of the Revolution composed of three members—Abd el Latíf Baghdadi, Hassan Ibrahim, and Anwar es Sadát. The Tribunal was empowered to try persons accused of high treason and other crimes involving the security of the state. Its trials could be either public or secret, as circumstances required, and there could be no appeal from its sentences. Each sentence, however, would be subject to ratification by the full Council of the Revolution, which would have the power either to increase or decrease it, according to the judgment of a majority of its members.

No one liked the Tribunal of the Revolution, and we abolished it, I am happy to say, as soon as we safely could. Between September 26, 1953, and June 30, 1954, the original Tribunal tried thirty-one cases. Four persons convicted of treasonable activities on behalf of the British were hanged. The death sentence passed against Ibrahim Abd el Hadi, the former Prime Minister, was commuted to life imprisonment. Mustafa en Nahass and certain other Wafdists were condemned but not sentenced for their moral guilt in condoning the misconduct of those Wafdists, including Serag ed Din, who were sentenced to long terms of imprisonment. Madame Nahass, the only woman who was tried, was also given a "moral" sentence and deprived of 322 acres of farmland worth LE 83,624 ($240,000)—the estimated illegal profit that she had made in rigging the Alexandria cotton market. Two of Faruk's cronies, Dr. Ahmed Nakíb, the former director of the Moassat Hospital in Alexandria, and "Brigadier" Mohammed Hilmi Hussein, were each convicted of corrupt practices and sentenced to fifteen years in prison. Mohammed Kamel el Kawísh, the former governor of Cairo, was given a fifteen-year suspended sentence. Four journalists were also convicted. Abul Kheir Naguib, the publisher of the weekly newspaper *El Gumhúr el Mussri* (*The Egyptian People*), was sentenced to life imprisonment. Mahmúd Abul Fath, the publisher of the daily *El Mussri* (*The Egyptian*), was tried in absentia (since he and his brother Ahmed had found it expedient to leave the country) and sentenced to ten years in prison. Their brother Hussein, the editor of *El Mussri*, who had not left Egypt, received a fifteen-year suspended sentence.

All of Mahmúd's possessions in Egypt, including his various publishing houses, were confiscated in lieu of his paying a fine of LE 354,438 ($1,017,237). This sum represented the illicit income that he was known to have received but which he had not declared, and on which he had paid no taxes. Abul Kheir Naguib (to whom I am not related) and the Abul Fath brothers were convicted of corrupt practices. But another charge against them was neither mentioned at their trial nor reported in the press— namely, that they had systematically slanted the news in the interests of Russia, from which country they had accepted subsidies in the guise of advertising on behalf of industrial and commercial enterprises in East Germany and other Russian colonies in Europe.

Mahmúd Shukri, a former *Mussri* reporter, was earlier convicted of treasonable activities on behalf of the British in the Suez Canal Zone. He was sentenced to ten years in prison.

VI

We waited for more than a year to take overt action against the Communists and their dupes for fear of weakening our case against the British. We may have been mistaken, but we felt that if we thus supported the West against the East before the British agreed to withdraw from Egypt we could never make them leave. H. G. Wells once referred despairingly to Neville Chamberlain's cabinet as a "limpet" government. Egyptians, with equal justice, might have referred to Britain's military squatters in the Canal Zone as a "limpet" occupation. It was useless to warn us of the peril of Russian imperialism so long as we were not permitted to rid ourselves of the barnacles of British imperialism clinging to the rusty hulk of an outworn system of strategy. You cannot make allies of people whom you insist on treating as colonial subjects. Neither can you make colonial subjects the enemies of your enemies unless you treat them as allies. Hence our reluctance to take action against the Communists in spite of the fact that we were well aware of their noxious influence.

Fortunately for the West, and unfortunately for the East, the

Communists in Egypt forced our hand. Instead of supporting the
Revolution, as they might have been expected to do, given their
humanitarian pretensions, they allied themselves with our other
enemies in an effort to frustrate our social, economic and political
reforms.

Most of the Communists in Egypt are of non-Egyptian origin.
The Greeks, Jews, and Armenians among them are far more
numerous than their Arabic adherents—a fact that limits their
importance in a predominantly Moslem country. They have made
considerable headway, even so, among the former Moslems
who constitute the so-called "intelligentsia." A typical representative of such creatures is Kamel el Bindari, "the Red Pasha," who
was once King Faruk's ambassador in Moscow. Bindari has been
useful to the Communists as the leader of the "Partisans of Peace,"
an organization that serves to gather recruits while hiding the
real purposes of the men behind it. Henri Curiel, the founder of
Haditu, the most powerful of the various Communist parties in
Egypt, fled to France before the Revolution. Most of his apostles,
including Fathi el Ramli, Yussef Hilmi, and Mary Rosenthal,
have since been arrested, tried, and convicted of subversion. So
have three Zionists with possible Communist connections—Victor
Levi, Hermann Nathanson, and Robert Nessím Dasa—who have
confessed to setting fire to books in the American libraries in Cairo
and Alexandria.

We did our best from the very beginning to remove the major
causes of Communism in Egypt—a corrupt monarchy, an inequitable system of land tenure, a general disregard for the rights
of labor, and a hated foreign occupation. So long as British troops
remained in the Canal Zone, however, we were denounced as
"agents of imperialism" every time we interfered with illegal
Communist activities. As Abd el Nasser remarked to an American

journalist on the eve of the second anniversary of the Revolution, "Only one major unwitting ally [of] Communism remains in Egypt—the British troops in the . . . Canal Zone, [whose presence] enables the Communists, disguised as nationalists, to stir up trouble and gain supporters." Now that the British have at long last agreed to evacuate the Canal Zone, the Communists have been deprived of the last remaining excuse for their existence. Provided the British evacuate their forces according to schedule, and refrain from exerting economic pressure on Egypt in the future, it will be less difficult from now on for us to keep our Communists under control.

But the Communists are not the only extremists who have attempted to destroy the Egyptian Revolution. The Moslem Brothers, instead of co-operating with the Liberation Rally, had joined it only to subvert it. On February 12, 1954, during a celebration of the first anniversary of the Sudan Agreement, a group of armed Moslem Brothers attacked a meeting of the Liberation Rally at Cairo University. A sound truck was burned and a score of students were wounded before order could be restored. It was not the first of such incidents, nor, as we were advised by the police, was it likely to be the last. We therefore abolished the Brotherhood, closed its meeting places, and arrested several hundreds of its leading members, including Hassan el Hudeibi, its "Supreme Guide," and Saleh el Ashmawi, the editor of *El Da'awa* (*The Call*), its official weekly newspaper. Hudeibi, Ashmawi, and most of the others have since been released and the Brotherhood has since been re-enfranchised—but only on condition that the organization confine itself to religious, cultural, and social affairs, and refrain from opposing the regime.[3]

[3]The Moslem Brotherhood was again abolished following the attempt on Abd el Nasser's life on October 26, 1954.

6

WHY I RESIGNED

"In the name of God, the Beneficent, the Merciful," I wrote, "I address myself to the gentlemen of the Council of the Revolution:

"After presenting my compliments, I regret to announce that, for reasons you will excuse me for not mentioning here, I can no longer carry out my duties in the manner I consider best calculated to serve the national interests. I must therefore ask you to accept my resignation from all the posts that I presently occupy, along with my thanks for the co-operation that each of you has so kindly given me during my term of office.

"I pray to Almighty God to help you in serving our country in the spirit of unity and co-operation."

Such was the text of the letter of resignation that I submitted on February 23, 1954. My differences with my junior colleagues were differences of tactics rather than of strategy. My experience as a Prime Minister had reinforced my conviction as a general that the efficiency of every organization, civilian or military, depends on a logical chain of command. Committee government, as I have already remarked, has certain strengths as well as weaknesses. Efficiency is not among them. The larger the committee the less efficient it is likely to be. A double committee is less efficient than a single committee, and a triple committee is less efficient still.

Egypt, at the time of my resignation, was being governed by a triple committee—an official cabinet, an unofficial cabinet, and a joint committee supposedly representing each. As the President, Prime Minister, and "Leader of the Revolution" (as I was described in the provisional Constitution), I was supposedly in control of each. Actually I was in control of none. Such control as existed was exercised by a majority of the Council of the Revolution.

Either of two things could be done. Either I could be given the power I needed to govern Egypt in what I considered the proper manner, or I could resign in favor of Abd el Nasser. The one thing that could not be done was to continue the way we were going. As the President, Prime Minister, and Leader of the Revolution, I was responsible for every action taken by the government. I had no objection to assuming responsibility for actions of which I approved. But I was no longer willing to assume responsibility for actions of which I could not approve or regarding which I was not consulted.

Abd el Nasser, for whom I have always had the greatest admiration and respect, is a young man of exceptional ability. I suggested that he allow me to run things for a few years until he had acquired the experience necessary to succeed me, at which time, I assured him, I would gladly resign in his favor. Otherwise, I said, I would be forced to resign immediately, even at the cost of creating a crisis, for I could no longer tolerate the anomalies of com-

mittee rule. It would be better for him to run things without my
help than for me to go on pretending to run things that were
actually being run by others in ways of which I could not approve.

I could neither appoint nor dismiss ministers without the approval of a majority of the members of the Council of the Revolution. Yet, as Prime Minister, I was obliged to support the acts of
my ministers whether I approved of them or not. I was also obliged
to approve the decisions of the new Commander in Chief of the
Armed Forces even though I was seldom consulted before it was
too late for me to do anything about them.

Although I believe in the doctrine of checks and balances, I do
not believe in divided responsibility. I was not asking for absolute
power. I was simply asking for the power necessary to live up to
my responsibilities. I was perfectly willing to consult the Council
regarding all of my decisions, and to bow to the will of the
majority, provided the Council, in turn, was willing to assume
responsibility for those decisions of which I could not approve.
This was not the same thing as asking for an unlimited veto. It was
simply asking for a limited veto that could be overridden on condition that the Council did so openly. It was right and necessary for
the Council's meetings to be secret. It was neither right nor necessary for me to be forced to assume the sole responsibility for decisions secretly taken by the Council against my better judgment.

I shall not ennumerate my specific differences with the Council
here. It is enough, I think, for me to say that most of them re-
volved around what Abd el Nasser has called the "philosophy"
of the Revolution. Perhaps, since neither of us is a philosopher, it
would be better to call it the "psychology" of the Revolution. Abd
el Nasser believed, with all the bravado of a man of thirty-six,
that we could afford to alienate every segment of Egyptian public
opinion, if necessary, in order to achieve our goals. I believed, with

all the prudence of a man of fifty-three, that we would need as much popular support as we could possibly retain. I further believed that it would be better to sacrifice, or at least delay, the attainment of some of our objectives in order to ensure the attainment of others. I believed, in short, that half a loaf was better than none. Abd el Nasser believed in taking greater risks than I thought were wise in an effort to obtain the whole loaf. It remains for the course of history to determine which of us was right. If I am proved wrong, and I am still alive, I shall be the first to congratulate Gamál on his superior judgment.

II

On the afternoon of February 23, after receiving my letter of resignation, Gamál Salem and Hussein el Shafei came to see me at my home. When I declined to withdraw my resignation, they insisted that I accompany them to the joint meeting of the cabinet and the Council of the Revolution that was being held that afternoon at the Chamber of Deputies. After a long discussion, we finally agreed to keep my letter of resignation a secret and to take no action until after I returned from Sudan. I would fly to Khartum with Saláh Salem, as planned, on February 28, to attend the inauguration of Sudan's provisional Parliament. In the meantime the Council of the Revolution would reconsider our differences and decide, within two weeks, whether to accept my resignation or to recognize the powers that went with my responsibilities as Prime Minister.

By the next day, however, I realized that the Council had changed its mind. Only four of the six military ministers attended my cabinet meeting that afternoon. Abd el Nasser and Saláh

Salem failed to appear. Gamál Salem and Baghdadi excused themselves after a few minutes, saying that they were tired; presently Kemál ed Din Hussein excused himself and a little later Zakaria Mohi ed Din followed his example. There was nothing to do but adjourn.

As I left the cabinet room to return to my office across the hall, I was surrounded by a group of journalists. They asked me why the others were meeting in my absence at the new headquarters in Gezira of the Council of the Revolution. I did my best to give the reporters a convincing explanation, but I could tell that they were not deceived. They knew as well as I did that a crisis was about to occur.

Saláh Salem had promised the day before to meet me in my office following the cabinet meeting to help me to select the presents that I was to give to various notables in Sudan. My civilian secretary, Saláh ed Din es Shehad, had assembled a large array of samples which I now proceeded to examine. Half an hour later, when Salem had not appeared, I decided to go home. On an impulse I told Shehad to clean out my desk and put my private papers and other personal belongings into the new suitcase that I had bought to take with me to Sudan. But then I changed my mind. It would be better, I decided, to leave my office as it was.

Just as I was about to leave, my military secretary, Major Ismail Faríd, appeared. He asked me to sign a paper authorizing a representative of the Council of the Revolution to buy my presents for me without bothering to compare the price and quality of the samples assembled in my office. I signed the paper on Faríd's assurance that its only purpose was to save time. If I waited to compare all the samples, he said, my presents would not be ready in time to take them with me to Khartum.

That night, before I went to bed, I asked my wife to remind me to call Faríd or Shehad in the morning. I had decided, on reflection, to rescind the authorization that I had signed and to purchase my presents in the prescribed manner. If they were not ready in time, it would make no difference; they could always be sent down to Khartum on a later airplane.

I awoke at six-thirty. At seven, after saying my prayers, I tried to call Faríd. Both my outside telephones were out of order. I then tried my third and last telephone, which was connected by a direct line to the Council of the Revolution. When I found that it, too, was out of order, I realized that I was under arrest.

I sent my servant Mohsen to see if the Republican Guards outside my house had been relieved. Mohsen came back frightened. He said that the Guards had been replaced by a mixed detachment of infantry and military police. A soldier had ordered him at the point of his bayonet to return to the house and stay there.

In the early days of the Revolution a barbed-wire fence had been erected around the immediate area in which I lived. I had opposed the measure on the ground that it was an inconvenience to those of my neighbors whose houses were inside the enclosure. My security advisers, however, had insisted on maintaining the fence and had even gone so far as to erect a number of pillboxes inside the enclosure—to protect my life, they said, in the event of an insurrection. No insurrection had occurred, of course, and, as events would prove, the enclosure failed to serve its purpose the only time it was ever tested.

I now sent my second servant, Bahder, to buy some kerosene. Our stoves were empty, and, unless he filled them, the cook would be unable to prepare a hot breakfast for the boys. But Bahder was not allowed to leave the compound, and the cook, who had been waiting outside the perimeter, was not allowed to enter.

Finally I sent a note to the captain commanding the military police. I suggested that he ask the Council of the Revolution whether my servants were to be allowed to enter and leave the compound and whether my sons were to be allowed to go to school. An hour later the captain replied that the boys would not be allowed to go to school and that the cook would not be allowed to enter. One servant, however, would be allowed to emerge from time to time for the sole purpose of providing my family and me with the necessities of life.

Annoyed though I was, I decided to treat my predicament as a joke. We had bought a calf in honor of my impending journey to Sudan. The meat was to be distributed, according to Moslem custom, among the poor. I now asked the captain to send for a butcher to kill the calf. When he refused to do so, I asked him to have the calf delivered to my brother-in-law, Mahmúd Labíb, with the request that he have it killed in my stead. But the captain, after consulting the Council, informed me that the calf, if it left the compound, would have to be sent to a "charitable organization." Inasmuch as my wife had already promised the animal's meat to a number of our poorer neighbors, I rejected his proposal. The calf, unaware of what was happening, now began to complain of hunger, and, for lack of anything more substantial to feed him, the boys gave him two quarts of milk, which they mixed from a can of powder in the kitchen.

At last the captain relented and allowed the cook to enter the compound. The cook butchered the calf, divided up the meat according to my wife's instructions, and, with the help of Mohsen and Bahder, smuggled it out in small packages to the house of my brother-in-law. Mahmúd had meanwhile been arrested. His wife, however, saw to it that the meat was delivered to the poor people for whom it was intended.

I was not supposed to see any newspapers, but several were later smuggled in to me, and from them as well as from the radio I was able to keep up with what was happening in Cairo.

That afternoon I took the first nap that I had been able to take in a long time. Later I spent several hours reading the Koran in order to prepare myself for the ordeal that was about to follow. Finally, as darkness fell, I opened my diary and began to jot down the events of the past few days. I introduced my remarks with the following quotation from the Koran: "Let us not forget the good things that were between us."

After bringing my diary up to date, I said my prayers and prepared to go to bed. But before I did I swore to God that I would endure everything, however painful, and accept every accusation and insult without offering a word in my own defense. I wanted, this time, to set another example for my fellow countrymen to follow. Egyptian politicians, in my opinion, have been far too prone to indulge in recriminations. I wanted to be an exception, for I knew that recriminations would only increase our differences and make it impossible for them to be repaired. I also knew that, after the heat of their anger had died away, my junior colleagues would regret their harsh words, and I wanted to be in a position to make peace with them as soon as they were ready to make peace with me. The Revolution was far too important to allow it to be jeopardized by my differences with Abd el Nasser.

III

The Revolution, according to a communiqué issued by my junior colleagues the next morning (February 25), had not been "carried out so that any individual or group of individuals should rise to power and be given privileges and honors. God is our

witness that the Revolution had no other aim than to provide a
sound foundation for the aspirations of a country that had suffered
greatly from the vices and corruption of the old regime. . . .

"What complicated the task of the Council of the Revolution
was [their determination] to present the people with a leader who
was more mature than they were and who came from outside their
organization. Because of his rank and age the choice fell upon
General Naguib, whose reputation . . . had not been tarnished
by the corruption of the old regime. General Naguib was advised
of our choice and accepted it two months before the Revolution
occurred.[1]

"[Later] a criticial situation arose from the fact that the . . .
Council of the Revolution [pursued its deliberations for over a
month] without the participation of General Naguib. In fact,
until 25 August, he did not belong to the Council of the Revolution, and it was only on that date that the Council decided to
admit him and appoint him its president after Lieutenant Colonel
Gamál Abd el Nasser—who had been nominated president of the
Council for the year ending 31 October 1952—had given up his
post in favor of General Naguib. . . .

"Six months had not elapsed before General Naguib began
to ask the Council to give him broader powers than those pos-
sessed by ordinary members. But the Council categorically refused
to depart from its statutes, which had been drawn up several years
before the Revolution, and which stipulated that all members
should be equal, including the president. The only exception was
a voting tie, in which event the president would have the right
to cast the deciding vote.

"Despite the fact that he was nominated to be President of the

[1]As I have already stated, I joined the Free Officers in the summer of 1949
and became their president in the spring of 1952.

republic as well as Prime Minister, president of the Council, and
president of the Joint Congress [of the cabinet and the Council],
General Naguib insisted that he be given broader powers than
those of the Council itself. But we maintained our refusal so that
we could assure a fair distribution of powers among the members
of the Council.[2]

"Recently General Naguib presented several precise demands
—that he be given the right to veto decisions . . . passed by the
Council, even though every decision was based on a majority vote;
to appoint and dismiss ministers; and to approve the promotion,
dismissal, and transfer of officers of the Armed Forces. In other
words, he demanded absolute individual powers. . . ."

Such was the Council's official version of what had happened.
It differed not only from my own version but also from the
partial versions of individual members of the Council. Actually,
as I have explained, I had not asked for powers that were any
greater than those normally given to the prime ministers and
presidents of modern constitutional republics. It is normal for the
President to be at least the nominal Commander in Chief of
the Armed Forces and to be given the right to approve the appointments and dismissals of officers. It is also normal for the
Prime Minister to be allowed to approve the appointments and
dismissals of high government officials, including chiefs of diplomatic missions, and to be allowed to dismiss from his cabinet
those ministers who refuse to give him their loyal co-operation.
In the absence of such powers, it becomes impossible to govern.
Someday, I hope, it will be possible for me to discuss this question
in greater detail. For the present, however, I must pass over many
things in silence.

[2]In other words, the ship of state was to be commanded by twelve captains
—eleven too many, in my opinion.

IV

At five-thirty on Saturday morning (February 27), I was awakened by a tapping on my bedroom window. I told whoever was tapping to come to the front door. My visitors consisted of eight cavalry officers headed by Major Khaled Mohi ed Din, the youngest member of the Council of the Revolution. Khaled took me aside and told me that the Council had decided to make him Prime Minister and to invite me to resume the office of President. If I accepted, he said, the other members of the Council would resign as a group in our favor.

Khaled was only thirty-one. The idea of making him the Prime Minister of Egypt was no more to my taste than the idea of the others' resigning. But all I said was that I would consider returning as President only if all the others, including Khaled, agreed to co-operate with me as before—"as comrades, if not as ministers."

Khaled and his friends left me to return to the Council of the Revolution. If all went well, they said, a communiqué announcing my return as President on my own conditions would be broadcast at seven o'clock. Shortly thereafter a delegation would arrive to escort me to the Palace of the Republic.

At six-thirty, however, I was abducted by two military police officers who took me to the headquarters of the artillery in Almaza. Anti-aircraft guns had been placed in a defensive circle around the compound. I soon discovered why. Large numbers of angry officers and men of all services had assembled outside to demand my release.

Among those present at the artillery headquarters was Captain Hassan Tuhami, a young intelligence officer, who told me that it had been discovered that Khaled Mohi ed Din and his followers were Communists. I refused to believe him, saying that I thought it would do nothing but harm to Egypt's reputation abroad if the Council of the Revolution attempted to besmirch my supporters in the cavalry, or any other branch of the Armed Forces, by means of such accusations. I suggested that the Council would do better to accuse me of treason and to shoot me, if necessary, in order to maintain the unity and good name of the military movement. I even offered to confess publicly to any charges that the Council might wish to prefer against me. But Tuhami rejected my proposal, insisting that my personal integrity was not in question.

I was presently removed through a back door and driven out into the desert. At first I thought my captors were going to murder me, but then I realized that they were simply trying to avoid an unequal battle between the Council's outnumbered supporters and my own. At last, full of apologies and promising that I would be set free in a matter of hours, they drove me home.

In the meantime, as I later learned, an official Sudanese delegation had flown up from Khartum with instructions not to return without me, or at least without a firm promise from the Council that I would be set free and allowed to retire to Sudan if I so desired. It was the hostile reaction of the Sudanese, I suppose, combined with the hostile reaction of the Egyptians themselves, that prompted my colleagues to insist on my resuming office as President if not as Prime Minister of Egypt. I was so associated in the people's minds with the Revolution, it seemed, that few Egyptians were willing to support it any longer without at least my tacit approval.

Later that morning I signed two messages that were delivered to me by emissaries of the Council of the Revolution:

In the first, before I had agreed to resume office as President,

I said that I considered it my duty "to explain to my brothers and sons, the Egyptians and the Arabs, that I resigned my various posts of my own accord, convinced that the Council of the Revolution is the natural body in which to concentrate our national interests and the sacred goals of the Egyptian Revolution. . . .

"I want to emphasize to my fellow countrymen that the Council's decision to accept my resignation was not intended to advance the interests of any individual or group of individuals and that the Council has striven at all times to advance the national interests and nothing but the national interests. . . .

"I therefore appeal to every sincere patriot not to use my name in vain. My resignation was not intended as merchandise to be bought and sold for personal advantage or to serve the interests of our enemies. . . ."

In the second message I said only that, "in order to maintain the unity of the nation in the present circumstances, I have accepted the invitation of the Council of the Revolution to resume the Presidency of the Egyptian Parliamentary Republic."

Both messages were published the following morning (February 28), together with a communiqué, signed by the Council, which read in part:

"The people have clearly expressed their desire to close their ranks . . . and advance as one caravan along the same road.

"In view of this demonstration of the people's feelings, [let] forgiveness fill all hearts and [let] everything be forgotten except the national interests and the need for reaching our destination, which is a sound democratic life, along the shortest possible road.

"The Council of the Revolution . . . in the name of the people . . . solemnly . . . [announces] that the caravan will continue on its way with . . . Mohammed Naguib in the van as the President of the Egyptian Parliamentary Republic.

"The Council of the Revolution, headed by . . . Gamál Abd
el Nasser [as Prime Minister], appeals to the Egyptians, the . . .
Sudanese, and the [other] friendly Arab and Oriental peoples
to help with all their . . . strength . . . to restore tranquillity
. . . so that the crisis through which the country has passed may
promptly be forgotten."

So it was Gamál and not Khaled who was to replace me as
Prime Minister. Khaled, in fact, was to be expelled from the
country and a number of his followers were to be placed on trial
as suspected Communists. The earlier decision to let him replace
me as Prime Minister had been either a trick or an act of despera-
tion.

Until I signed the messages from which I have quoted, the
streets around my house had been cordoned off in the hope of preventing a demonstration in my favor. I could tell, however, from
the distant roar of men's voices, punctuated by the traditional
zaghalít, or trill, of festive women, that a sizable crowd was
gathering. At last it broke through the cordon and besieged the
barbed-wire fence around my compound. The excitement of the
crowd soon grew to such a pitch that it could no longer be controlled. Together with my guards, I found it necessary to retreat
to the house of a neighbor as the crowd broke through the barbed-
wire fence and forced its way into my own house in the hope of
congratulating me in person. My wife and servants did their best
to calm the crowd, announcing that I would appear at the Republican Palace in the morning.

It was not until 1 A.M., after the last remnants of the crowd had
dispersed, that I was able to return home and go to bed. The
house was a mess, but no serious damage had been done and
nothing at all had been stolen. I was as grateful for as I was
astonished by the crowd's unprecedented restraint.

At nine-thirty that morning (February 28), I was driven to the Republican Palace, where, from its balcony overlooking the square, I addressed the largest crowd that I have ever seen assembled. I attempted to minimize the crisis, which I described as "a summer cloud that had quickly passed away," and to restore unity by urging "all sincere Egyptians" to support "their brothers and mine—the members of the Council of the Revolution."

Although I suggested "Forgive and Forget" as our motto for the day, the Wafdists, Communists, and Moslem Brothers had already succeeded in spoiling the celebration. In order to exploit my differences with the Council for their own ends, they had incited two riots that very morning. In Giza, on the campus of Cairo University, eight students had been killed and twenty had been wounded. A little later a policeman and a student had been killed and fifteen others had been wounded when a mob formed in front of the Semiramis Hotel. Now, as I spoke, I could see the Moslem Brothers waving bloodstained handkerchiefs in the faces of the crowd below me. One of their leaders, Abd el Kader Oda, interrupted my speech to demand an immediate investigation of the riots.

"I have returned as President," I replied, "on the understanding that ours shall be a parliamentary republic."

When Oda continued to interrupt me, I invited him to join me on the balcony. Later, after I had promised to investigate the riots, he ordered his followers to disperse.

v

Early the next morning I flew to Khartum with Saláh Salem only to be greeted by another riot in which twenty-two people, including H. Sutherland McGuigan, the British chief of police, were killed, and 177 others were wounded. The British authorities had allowed the Umma (Nation) Party to organize outside the airport a demonstration in favor of independence from both Egypt and Great Britain. Instead of driving into Khartum in an open car at the head of a pro-Egyptian procession, as it had been arranged for me to do, I was whisked away in a closed car and driven straight to the palace of the British Governor General, Sir Robert Howe. The Governor General's excuse for the extraordinary treatment accorded me was that he had been obliged to protect my life, which, so far as I could tell, had never been in danger.

The riot occurred just before noon following a demonstration in front of the Governor General's Palace. I could probably have prevented the bloodshed had I been allowed to address the crowd or even to telephone to the Umma leader, El Sayed Sir Abd er Rahmán el Mahdi, with whom, despite our political differences, I have always enjoyed the most friendly personal relations. Unfortunately the British chose to "protect my life" to the extent of treating me more as a prisoner than as a guest. I was cut off every time I tried to telephone to the Mahdi and other political leaders, and in the end I had to communicate with them through intermediaries. The Mahdi told my Sudanese military aide, Major General Ali el Banna, that he had planned a banquet in my honor following the demonstration, the only purpose of which was to impress me with the strength of his following. After shouting such slogans as "No British, No Egyptians," and "Sudan for the Sudanese," the crowd, when I was not allowed to appear, began to cheer me personally, shouting, "You are safe, Naguib; you are in the hands of God."

The demonstrators were mostly primitive tribesmen armed

with spears, knives, and clubs. They began to riot only after the unarmed police attempted to disperse them with tear gas, a substance with which they were not familiar, and which they naturally mistook for a lethal weapon.

Selwyn Lloyd, the British Minister of State, who had come to Khartum to attend the inaugural ceremonies, joined me in one of the palace halls. As we paced the floor together, he warned me to be careful lest I be killed. I expressed the opinion that, as a Briton, his life was in greater danger than mine. I also expressed my regret that the Governor General had not seen fit to let me telephone to the Mahdi in an effort to put a stop to the riot, which need never have occurred had the British taken the precautions they normally took on such occasions.

Disgusted by what had been allowed to happen, and convinced that the British were by no means as innocent as they pretended to be, I flew back to Cairo with Saláh Salem early the next morning.

The Council of the Revolution in my absence had arrested several hundred persons accused of exploiting my differences with Abd el Nasser in the hope of producing a counterrevolution. That night I delivered a radio address in which I deplored the Khartum riot. I also issued a warning to the Egyptian people to beware of the opportunists who were attempting to exploit my name in order to destroy the Revolution.

Three days later we abolished censorship once again and announced that a constituent assembly would be created in time to hold its first meeting on July 23, 1954, the second anniversary of the Revolution. The function of the assembly would be to revise and ratify the new Constitution and to act as a provisional parliament until a new Chamber of Deputies could be elected.

On March 9, after a joint meeting of the cabinet and the

Council of the Revolution, I agreed to resume my posts as Prime Minister and Leader of the Revolution until such time as we could hold a free election. As I explained the next evening, at a banquet given in my honor by Abd el Hakím Amer, four facts had emerged from the unhappy events of the past few days. First of all, we had shown our enemies that the Egyptian Revolution was supported not only by the great majority of Egyptians but also by Arabs and Moslems everywhere and especially by our brothers of the Nile Valley, the Sudanese. The second fact was that the people had instinctively realized that our strongest weapon was unity and that dissension could no longer be tolerated. The third was that the people had made it clear that they wished us to proceed forthwith to fulfill our promise to free them from the last vestiges of oppression. The fourth fact was that dissension among ourselves had led in turn to disorders among the people. These facts constituted lessons, I felt, that we should all take to heart.

VI

Events now moved rapidly toward an unexpected climax. It had never been my intention to disband the Council of the Revolution or to restore the old political parties. Still less had I intended to call a halt to the Egyptian Revolution. All I had intended to do was to gain popular support for the movement by gradually demilitarizing the government, creating a constituent assembly, and holding a referendum to prepare the Egyptian people for a free election at some future date.

We would have risked very little and gained a great deal, I think, if we had held the sort of referendum that I proposed. While it was far from being the free election that we had promised, it was at least a step in that direction; and the people, I am sure, would have welcomed an opportunity to register the extent of their approval of the agrarian reforms and other aspects of the Egyptian Revolution.

Instead of supporting my proposal, a majority of the Council voted on March 25 to issue the following communiqué, which had been drafted by Abd el Nasser:

"1. The Council of the Revolution will surrender its powers to a constituent assembly on 24 July 1954, at which time it will proclaim the end of the Egyptian Revolution.

"2. The political parties that have been abolished [including the Moslem Brotherhood] are hereby permitted to resume their activities.

"3. [In spite of reports to the contrary], the Council of the Revolution will not form a new political party.[3]

"4. All citizens from this date enjoy full political freedom.

"5. The constituent assembly will be formed by means of a free and direct election; none of its members will be appointed.[4]

"6. The first task of the constituent assembly, which will hold its first meeting on 23 July 1954, will be to elect the President of the Republic."

I was thus outmaneuvered by Abd el Nasser and my junior colleagues. Faced with only two alternatives—either to vote in favor of the foregoing communiqué or to vote in favor of continuing the military dictatorship without change until the end of

[3]Abd el Nasser had earlier announced that he and the other Free Officers would resign from the Armed Forces in order to form what was to have been called the Social Republican Party.

[4]According to my proposal, sixty of its 300 members would have been appointed. No one found guilty of corrupt practices would have been eligible either to be elected or appointed to the constituent assembly. The Council of the Revolution would have continued to function as a presidential advisory council until the end of the transitional period.

the three-year period of transition—I voted in favor of issuing the communiqué. It was far from what I wanted, as everybody knew, but it created the effect desired by Abd el Nasser: it so shocked the supporters of the Revolution that the Liberation Rally, on March 28, was able to organize a general strike that amounted, in effect, to a second coup d'état.

I resigned again as Prime Minister on April 17 in favor of Abd el Nasser, who proceeded to form a cabinet in which eight instead of six of my junior colleagues would be ministers. On September 1, after initialing the draft of the Suez Agreement, he reshuffled the cabinet in such a way as to include every one of the eleven remaining members of the Council of the Revolution except myself. Gamál Salem, who resigned as Minister of Communications in favor of Fathi Radwan, previously a Minister of State and a former civilian Minister of National Guidance, now became Vice-Prime Minister. Abd el Latíf Baghdadi, who had become the Minister of Municipal Affairs, was succeeded as Minister of War first by Hussein el Shafei and then by Abd el Hakím Amer, who remained Commander in Chief of the Armed Forces. Kemál ed Din Hussein, who was succeeded as Minister of Social Affairs by Hussein el Shafei, became the new Minister of Education. Anwar es Sadát, who remained the director of the daily *El Gumhuría* (*The Republic*) and other official and semi-official publications, now became a Minister of State. Saláh Salem remained the Minister of National Guidance and Minister of State for Sudanese Affairs and Zakaria Mohi ed Din remained the Minister of Interior. Hassan Ibrahim, for his part, remained in the new post created for him in April—that of Minister of State for Presidential Affairs. As such he has acted as my deputy and principal liaison officer with the cabinet and the Council. As for myself, I have remained in office as President and nominal Leader of the

Revolution in order to maintain a semblance of the unity that Egypt needs so badly.

Under the new military government censorship was reimposed; the universities were reorganized in order to curb the political extremism of their students; all political parties except the Moslem Brotherhood (whose leaders promised to behave themselves) were again abolished; and the leaders of two secret opposition groups were placed on trial and convicted of conspiring to overthrow the Council of the Revolution.

The first to be tried were sixteen cavalry officers headed by Captain Ahmed Ali Hassan el Mussri. All were charged with "attempting to incite a mutiny in the Armed Forces with the object of overthrowing the present regime by force." Mussri was sentenced on June 22 to fifteen years in prison. Eleven others were sentenced to from one to ten years; one was dishonorably discharged from the Army; and three were acquitted.

All were alleged to be followers of Khaled Mohi ed Din, who has since been removed from the Council of the Revolution and banished from Egypt. Yussef Saddík Mansúr, who had previously been removed from the Council, but who returned from exile prior to the crisis, is now in prison. Both Saddík and Khaled Mohi ed Din are accused by my colleagues of being Communists. They are further accused, along with Mussri and the others who were convicted, of having attempted to exploit my differences with Abd el Nasser in order to overthrow the present regime and establish a dictatorship of their own. Their guilt or innocence can be determined only by judicial procedure, and, until they have been tried, I shall refrain from making any comments.

Since my name has been connected with what is alleged to have been a Communist plot, however, I must reiterate that my differences with Abd el Nasser were differences of tactics rather than of strategy and were at all times in the nature of a family quarrel. Our common belief in the Egyptian Revolution—one objective of which is to remove the causes of Communism—has never once been an issue between us. The only issue was how we could best achieve our goals. If the Communists, Wafdists, or Moslem Brothers attempted to take advantage of my position during the crisis, they did so without my knowledge or consent and must pay the penalty, without expecting any sympathy from me, for any illegal activities in which they may have engaged.

Twenty-five civilians were also placed on trial. They were all members of the so-called "Democratic Party," and were headed by Mustafa Kemál Sidki, a former major who had been discharged from the Army on suspicion of being a Communist agent. The Democratic Party's immediate purpose, according to the indictment, was "to overthrow the present regime by force." Its ultimate purpose, however, was "to nationalize the means of production through the creation in Egypt of a social structure similar to that which exists in Russia by the same . . . methods as those used by Lenin and Stalin . . . [namely, by] inciting workers to strike and attack others, [thereby creating such] hatred of the propertied classes . . . as to [menace the maintenance of] public order." Three were acquitted and twenty-two were sentenced on September 2 to prison terms of from one to ten years. Sidki and Mary Rosenthal, whom I have mentioned earlier, were both sentenced to five years in prison.

7

EGYPT AND THE WEST

"If the reader will look at a map of the Nile system, he cannot fail to be struck by its resemblance to a palm-tree. At the top the green and fertile area of the Delta spreads like the graceful leaves and foliage. The stem is perhaps a little twisted, for the Nile makes a vast bend in flowing through the desert. South of Khartoum the likeness is again perfect, and the roots of the tree begin to stretch deeply into the Soudan. I can imagine no better illustration of the intimate and sympathetic connection between Egypt and the southern provinces. The water—the life of the Delta—is drawn from the Soudan, and passes along the channel of the Nile, as the sap passes up the stem of the tree, to produce a fine crop of fruit above. The benefit to Egypt is obvious; but Egypt does not benefit alone. The advantages of the connection are mutual; for if the Soudan is thus naturally and geographically an integral part of Egypt, Egypt is no less essential to the development of the Soudan. Of what use would the roots and the rich soil be, if the stem were severed, by which alone their vital essence may find expression in the upper air?

"Here, then, is a plain and honest reason for the [reconquest of Sudan]. To unite territories that could not indefinitely have continued divided; to combine peoples whose future welfare is inseparably intermingled; to collect energies which, concentrated, may promote a common interest; to join together what could not improve apart—these are the objects which, history will pronounce, have justified the enterprise. . . ."[1]

The passage just quoted is the most succinct statement of the Egyptian thesis regarding the unity of the Nile Valley that I have ever read. Its author, however, is not an Egyptian; he is an Englishman named Winston S. Churchill. As a politician, I fancy, Churchill has often had cause to regret the fact that his own words are the best possible refutation of the illogical position so long defended by his government. But as a journalist and historian he was too honest to deny the realities of Great Britain's position in Egypt and Sudan. He even went so far as to point out, in the same chapter of the same book, that "the cost to the British taxpayer of the recovery and part acquisition of the Soudan, of the military prestige, and of the indulgence of the sentiment known as 'the avenging of Gordon' has therefore been £800,000 [then about $4,000,000]; and it may be stated in all seriousness that English history does not record any instance of so great a national satisfaction being more cheaply obtained. The rest of the money has been provided by Egypt; and this strange country, seeming to resemble the camel, on which so much of her wealth depends, has, in default of the usual sources of supply, drawn upon some fifth stomach for nourishment, and, to the perplexity even of those best

[1] Cf. *The River War: An Account of the Reconquest of the Sudan* (London, 1899 and 1951), pp. 363–64.

acquainted with her amazing financial constitution, has stood the strain. . . ."[2]

My maternal grandfather and three of his brothers, as I have said, were killed in the same battle in which Gordon lost his life. My father and my uncle were Egyptian Army officers employed in the Sudan civil service, and my brother Ali and I grew up in Sudan and spent a large part of our lives in the service of what was supposed to have been a condominium, but which, until 1953, was a British colony disguised as a protectorate.

Although I am an Egyptian and not a Sudanese, I naturally have a tender feeling for the land in which I was born and in which so much of my family's blood was shed. It gave me great pleasure, therefore, to be able to create the conditions necessary for supplanting the inequitable and unworkable Agreement of 1899 with the equitable and eminently workable Agreement of 1953. In the preparation of this agreement I was greatly aided not only by Saláh Salem but also by Group Captain Hussein Zulfikar Sabri, the elder brother of Ali Sabri, who had served for years with the Egyptian Army in Sudan and who is now the Egyptian representative on the Governor General's Commission. Our predecessors had always assumed that Great Britain's insistence on protecting Sudan's right to "self-determination" was merely an excuse for depriving Egypt of its right to a say in how Sudan's future should be determined. And indeed, so long as Egypt was ruled by a King whose realm, in theory, included Sudan as well as Egypt, it was impossible for them to play what they could not but regard as a British game. It seemed to me, however, that, having rid ourselves of a King who had been as unpopular in Sudan as he had been in Egypt, we could beat the

[2]Ibid., p. 362. According to Churchill, Egypt's contribution to the cost of the war was £1,554,354, or almost twice as much as Britain's contribution.

British at their own game simply by calling their bluff. I accordingly reopened the negotiations that Hilali had suspended, and, on February 12, 1953, with the approval of the Council of the Revolution, I signed the agreement already mentioned. Its thirteen articles may be summarized as follows:

1. In order to permit the Sudanese to determine their future "in a free and neutral atmosphere," a three-year period of transition shall be established.

2. The Anglo-Egyptian condominium shall end on the same day as the period of transition, the question of sovereignty meanwhile being held in abeyance.

3. The Governor General, with the aid of an international commission, shall act as "the supreme constitutional authority" until the end of the transitional period.

4. The Governor General's Commission shall consist of five members—two Sudanese, one Egyptian, one Briton, and one Pakistani.

5. No act of the Governor General shall conflict in any way with the joint Anglo-Egyptian policy of maintaining "the unity of . . . Sudan as a single territory."

6. The Governor General shall be free to disregard the advice of his commission in matters concerning external affairs, changes in the self-government statute requested by the provisional Sudanese Parliament, and in any disputed matter if both the Egyptian and British governments within one month decide in favor of the Governor General.

7. In order to guarantee the holding of a free election before the end of the transitional period, a mixed electoral commission shall be established. It shall consist of seven members—three Sudanese, one Egyptian, one Briton, one American, and one Indian.

8. In order to provide "the free and neutral atmosphere requisite for self-determination," a Sudanization commission shall be established. It shall consist of five voting members—three Sudanese, one Egyptian, and one Briton—as well as one or more advisory members.

9. The period of transition shall end as soon as possible and on any day specified by the permanent Sudanese Parliament following its election according to the law to be drafted by the constituent assembly. In no event shall the transitional period last for more than three years.

10. Whenever the provisional Sudanese Parliament so resolves, the Egyptian and British governments shall draft the necessary law for the election of the constituent assembly. The election shall be held under international supervision.

11. Great Britain and Egypt shall withdraw their military forces from Sudan within three months of the day they are requested to do so by the permanent Sudanese Parliament.

12. The constituent assembly shall "decide the future of . . . Sudan as one integral whole" and shall draw up a Constitution and a law for the election of the permanent Sudanese Parliament. In deciding the future of Sudan, it shall vote either for complete independence or for some link "in any form" with Egypt.

13. Great Britain and Egypt shall "undertake to respect the decision of the constituent assembly concerning the future status" of Sudan.

II

The agreement, as I said at the time, opened a new page in Egypt's relations with Sudan. It also opened a new page in Egypt's relations with Great Britain and the United States. In October 1952, following the example of France, the United States established quasi-diplomatic relations with Sudan by means of a "liaison officer" accredited to the Governor General in Khartum. The agreement made it possible for the United States to use its influence more effectively in persuading Great Britain to negotiate with Egypt on a basis of equality. The agreement also made it possible for Pakistan and India to establish quasi-diplomatic relations with Sudan through their representatives on the Governor General's and electoral commissions. Thus, though the agreement embodied a number of concessions on Egypt's part, it so ventilated the Anglo-Egyptian dispute that Great Britain was no longer able to treat Egypt's representatives in Sudan as if they were poachers on a private British preserve. Sudan itself was henceforth to be treated as something more than a geographical expression, and, following the election of the provisional Parliament in December 1953, it was to be treated by all the powers concerned as a state in fact if not yet a state in law.

On October 29, 1952, in order to facilitate the Anglo-Egyptian Agreement, I had signed an informal agreement with all of the existing parties in Sudan, including the Umma, which was supposedly the strongest and most anti-Egyptian of them all. According to this preliminary agreement, Egypt would recognize Sudan's right to complete independence and would withdraw its objections to the self-government statute enacted by the British-controlled legislative assembly. The Sudanese parties, in return, would support Egypt's insistence on the establishment of two international commissions—one to advise the British Governor General and another to supervise the election of both the provisional and permanent Sudanese Parliaments.

Once I had come to terms with all the parties, I decided to

do what I could to unite and thereby strengthen those that supported Egypt's point of view. Until November 2, 1952, the pro-Egyptian elements in Sudan had been divided into no fewer than eight different parties. It was now agreed to unite them into a single National Union Party that would be strong enough to defeat the pro-British coalition dominated by the Umma. The National Unionists, who were themselves a coalition, agreed to accept the leadership of Ismail el Azhari, the president of the Ashigga (Fraternal) Party. Whereas Abdullah Khalil and the other leaders of the Umma were mostly followers of El Sayed Sir Abd er Rahmán el Mahdi, the leader of the Ansar sect of Islam, Azhari and the other leaders of the National Unionists were mostly followers of El Sayed Sir Ali el Mirghani, the leader of the Khatmía sect of Islam.[3]

The elections of November and December 1953 would decide whether the provisional Parliament was to be led by a representative of the pro-Egyptian coalition that was loyal to the Mirghani or a representative of the pro-British coalition that was loyal to the Mahdi.

The British, who had previously convinced themselves that the divided pro-Egyptian parties were no match for the Umma, now began to hedge their subsidies. Fearful that the National Unionists, under the impetus of the Egyptian Revolution, would develop new-found strength in the advocacy of a Sudanese republic in

[3]Ali el Mirghani is the Mahdi's principal rival for the religious leadership of the Moslem majority in Sudan. As the leader of the Khatmía, he opposes the political as well as the religious policies of the Mahdi, who at one time was suspected of aspiring to become the king of an independent Sudan in close relations with Great Britain. Abd er Rahmán, the present Mahdi, is a son of the original *Mahdi el Muntazar* (Awaited Guide), Mohammed Ahmed, who founded the Ansar and led the revolt against Egyptian rule that resulted in the so-called River War and the eventual British occupation of Sudan.

close relations with the Egyptian republic, they began to support the Social Republican Party headed by Ibrahim Yussef Bedri. They also created a number of minor parties designed to protect the pagans of the south, or so the British said, from the "rapacity" of the Moslems of the north. Thanks to the Anglo-Egyptian Agreement of 1953, however, we were able to prevent the British from openly encouraging the secession of the south, which might otherwise have been annexed, in accordance with an old British plan, to the protectorate of Uganda.

Since both the pro-British and pro-Egyptian coalitions favored the creation of an independent Sudanese republic, neither independence nor republicanism was a vital issue in the elections of 1953. The only real issue, which the British did their best to distort, was whether the new independent Sudanese republic should establish closer relations with Egypt than with Britain. The British effort to divide the Sudanese by supporting the pagan southerners against the Moslem northerners succeeded only in uniting the northerners behind the pro-Egyptian National Unionists. The accusation that the National Unionists were being subsidized by Egypt also did more harm than good from the British point of view. Since everybody knew that the Mahdi and the Umma had long been enjoying British subsidies, and that the Social Republicans as well as the various southern parties were also being financed by Britain, nobody took the accusation very seriously.

The elections, which resulted in an overwhelming victory for the National Unionists, repudiated the old British theory of Western tutelage and vindicated the new Egyptian theory of unity in independence. Previous Egyptian governments had failed to win the support of a majority of the Sudanese because of their insistence on the tutelage of a hated Egyptian monarchy. The Egyptian republic easily won the majority's support because it was willing to recognize Sudan's right to independence even though it continued to advocate the principle of unity. The Sudanese knew that the new Egypt, while eager to unify the Nile Valley, was prepared to deal with the new Sudan on a basis of equality.

In spite of British predictions to the contrary, the National Unionists won fifty-four of the ninety-seven seats in the Lower House of Parliament. The Umma candidates won only twenty seats, while the Social Republicans, who won only five, decided henceforth to vote with the National Unionists. The National Unionists also won twenty-two of the thirty elective seats in the Senate, of whose fifty members twenty were appointed by the Governor General. The Umma candidates won only three elective seats and the Social Republicans none.

On January 6, 1954, Ismail el Azhari was duly elected the first Prime Minister of Sudan. Three days later, in accordance with the Anglo-Egyptian Agreement of 1953, the British Governor General, Sir Robert Howe, proclaimed the beginning of the three-year period of transition. On January 9, 1957, if not before then, Sudan will become a sovereign state. In the meantime its government will be completely Sudanized and the British employees of the old administration will be retired.[4] Whenever its provisional Parliament so decides, the transitional period will be brought to an end, a constitutent assembly will be elected, and the assembly will vote for either complete independence or some sort of union with Egypt. One standing proposal, which the National Unionists seem inclined to favor, provides for complete independence in all but such matters of common interest as finance, defense, and

---

[4]In view of the poverty of the new Sudanese Government, individual Egyptians as well as individual Sudanese of all classes have been contributing to the public subscription necessary to pay the severance fees demanded by the departing British, who have also demanded and been granted generous pensions.

foreign affairs, the control of which would be shared with Egypt in the common interests of both countries.

III

The favorable outcome of the Sudanese elections made it possible for the United States to persuade Great Britain to resume negotiations for the withdrawal of its troops from the Suez Canal Zone. So long as the British found it possible to believe that the Sudanese depended on them for protection against the Egyptians, they could always persuade themselves, without any help from anyone, that the time was not yet ripe for an equitable Suez agreement. Once the Sudanese had conclusively demonstrated that they were as eager as their Egyptian brothers to say good-by to their unwelcome guardians, however, it was impossible even for the British not to read the writing on the wall. But, though they could read the writing, they were exceedingly reluctant to draw the obvious conclusion—namely, that their days were numbered in both Egypt and Sudan because their rule had been weighed and found wanting. At the Washington Conference in the summer of 1953, the British extracted a promise from the Americans to extend no military or economic assistance to Egypt until the Suez negotiations had been completed. At the Washington Conference of 1954, after a year of unnecessary delays, they were told that the United States was not prepared to wait indefinitely. Great Britain must either come to terms with Egypt or the United States would do so separately. Sir Winston Churchill, in spite of his age, proved once again that he was big enough to accept the inevitable. Orders were given to resume the negotiations, this time in earnest, and within a month both parties had initialed a draft agreement that could and should have been signed not later than 1946.[5]

"Many of the failures of British statesmanship," the late Duff Cooper (Viscount Norwich) observed, "have been due to the reluctance of Ministers to deal with a problem so long as postponement was possible. Too often have we been forced in the end to accept an unsatisfactory and even a humiliating solution because we have refused at the beginning to agree to a far better one. Too often have we conceded grudgingly and too late much more than would have been accepted gladly and gratefully at an earlier date."[6]

The Suez Agreement of 1954, while not unfavorable to Britain, was less favorable than it might have been if the British had not waited so long to face the fact that their strategical position throughout the entire Middle East was hopelessly out of date. The first atomic bomb was exploded over Hiroshima in 1945, but it was not until 1954, two years after the experimental explosion of the first hydrogen bomb, that the Prime Minister of Great Britain was willing to admit that "you can't maintain prestige with folly." Later, in defending the Suez Agreement in the House of Commons, he went on to admit "how utterly out of all proportion the Suez Canal and the position which we hold in Egypt are to the appalling developments and the appalling spectacles which imagination raises before us. Merely to try to imagine in outline and to portray the first few weeks of a war as it would be now . . . merely to portray that picture and submit it to the House would, I am sure, convince it of the obsolescence of the base and of the sense of proportion

[5]The final agreement, consisting of thirteen articles, two annexes, and eleven exchanges of letters, was signed on October 19, 1954.
[6]Cf. *Old Men Forget* (London, 1954), pp. 99–100.

which is vitally needed at the present time, not only in military dispositions but in all our attempts to establish human relationships between the nations."

If I were a Briton, I could think of better reasons than the hydrogen bomb for getting out of Egypt, but, if the hydrogen bomb was what convinced Sir Winston, I am content to let the matter stand—so long as the British keep their word and withdraw their troops according to schedule. I may perhaps be forgiven, though, if, as an Egyptian, I confess to a certain skepticism regarding British promises. During seventy-two years of total or partial occupation, the British have formally promised to restore Egypt's independence on at least eighty-six occasions.[7] Yet, until the Agreement of 1954 was initialed, Great Britain took the position that Egypt must first agree to some sort of military alliance before it could safely evacuate the Suez Canal Zone. The Council of the Revolution, for its part, took the position that Egypt would have to be given its independence before it could agree to any sort of alliance with the West. The government of an occupied country, as I have often remarked in public, is no more able to negotiate a treaty of alliance with the government of an occupying power—or, for that matter, with an allied power like the United States—than a prisoner is able to negotiate with his jailers, or their intermediaries, the terms of his parole. And negotiation, as the British well know, is essential to every alliance worthy of its name. I must therefore say to our British and American friends: Give us our freedom before you invite us to negotiate an alliance

[7] Cf. Jon Kimche, *Seven Fallen Pillars* (New York, 1953), p. 78. "As far back as 1911," Kimche writes, "a British author had published an anthology of British promises to Egypt; there were seventy-five unfulfilled undertakings to grant full independence. In the years that followed another dozen or so similar promises had been made. . . . And each time had come the sordid awakening. The Egyptians were willing to be fooled eighty-six times, but not eighty-seven."

with the West. And please don't expect us to sign an alliance until we can do so as free and equal partners.

The ten main articles of the "heads of agreement" initialed on July 27, 1954, may be summarized as follows:

1. With a view to "establishing Anglo-Egyptian relations on a new basis of mutual understanding and firm friendship," the Treaty of 1936 shall be supplanted by a new agreement along the following lines:

2. The agreement will last for seven years. During the last of these seven years "the two governments will consult together to decide what arrangements are necessary upon the termination of the agreement."

3. "Parts of the present . . . base will be kept in efficient working order . . . and capable of immediate use in accordance with the following paragraph.

4 (a). "In the event of an armed attack by an outside power" on Egypt, any member of the League of Arab States, or Turkey, "Egypt will afford to the United Kingdom such facilities as may be necessary" to reactivate the base and place it on a war footing.

(b). "In the event of a threat of an attack on any of the above-mentioned countries, there shall be immediate consultation between the United Kingdom and Egypt."

5. The base will be reorganized in accordance with Annex One.

6. "The United Kingdom will be accorded the right to move any British material into or out of the base at its discretion," but there will be no increase in the quantity of such material without the consent of the Egyptian Government.

7. "Her Majesty's forces will be completely withdrawn from Egyptian territory . . . within . . . twenty months from the date of signature of this agreement. The Egyptian Government

will afford all necessary facilities for the movement of men and
material in this connection."

8. This agreement, while recognizing that the Suez Canal "is
an integral part of Egypt," will not affect the Convention of
1888, whereby freedom of passage through the canal is guaranteed.[8]

9. The Egyptian Government will afford overflying, landing,
and servicing facilities for British military aircraft, which will receive most-favored-nation treatment.

10. Further questions of detail "will be settled by friendly
agreement in negotiations which will begin forthwith."

The following is a summary of the six points of Annex One:

1. "Her Majesty's Government shall have the right to maintain certain agreed installations and to operate them for current
requirements. . . . Her Majesty's Government . . . will discuss
with the Egyptian Government the disposal of any installation
which they no longer require. . . .

---

[8]The Convention of 1888 is not to be confused with the Act of Concession
of 1856, as revised in 1863, which regulates the status of the Suez Canal
Company. The concession will terminate on November 17, 1968, at which
time the Egyptian Government will exercise its right to buy up all of the
company's outstanding shares. The Convention of 1888 was a military
agreement between Great Britain, Germany, Austria-Hungary, Spain,
France, Italy, The Netherlands, Russia, and Turkey, Egypt then being a
Turkish possession. It stipulates that "the Suez Maritime Canal shall always
be free and open, in time of war as in time of peace, to every vessel of
commerce or of war, without distinction of flag. Consequently, the High
Contracting Parties agree not in any way to interfere with the free use of
the Canal, in time of war as in time of peace. The Canal shall never be
subjected to the exercise of the right of blockade." Inasmuch as Great
Britain has freely exercised the right of blockade in two World Wars,
however, Egypt's right to exercise the blockade against Israel has not been
seriously challenged. As Hugh J. Schonfield has observed, "it could by
no means be foreseen at the time what extraordinary political changes
would take place in the next sixty years, which if they did not make the
Convention a dead letter clearly demonstrated the need for drastic revision
of its terms." (Cf. *The Suez Canal in World Affairs* [London, 1952], p. 52.)

2. "Following the withdrawal of Her Majesty's forces the Egyptian Government will assume responsibility for the security of the base and of all equipment contained therein. . . .

3. "Her Majesty's Government will conclude contracts with one or more British or Egyptian commercial firms for the upkeep and operation of the installations referred to [above]. . . . These commercial firms will have the right to engage British and Egyptian civilian technicians and personnel; the number of the British technicians employed . . . shall not exceed a figure which shall be agreed upon in the detailed negotiations. . . .

4. "The Egyptian Government will give full support to the commercial firms referred to [above] . . . and will designate an authority with whom the contractors can co-operate for the discharge of their duties.

5. "The Egyptian Government will maintain in good order such installations, public utilities, communications, bridges, pipelines, and wharves, etc., as will be handed over to it according to the agreement between the two Governments. . . .

6. "Her Majesty's Government will be afforded facilities for the inspection of the installations referred to [above]. . . ."

The draft agreement initialed on July 27, 1954, differed from the draft agreement that neither side was willing to sign on October 21, 1953 (when negotiations were suspended), only in these respects:

Great Britain would have evacuated its combat troops in fifteen instead of twenty months. But 4000 British technicians would have been left behind to maintain the base for another period of three years and three months, at the end of which a third period of two and a half years would begin, making a total of seven years. During the third period Great Britain would have completed the dismantling of the base and reduced the number of its technicians from 4000 to 1000 and finally to 500. The agreement was never signed because the British insisted (1) that their technicians be allowed to wear military uniforms and (2) that they be allowed to reactivate the base at any time during the seven-year period in the event of an armed attack by an outside power on Egypt, any member of the League of Arab States, or Turkey or Iran. Seven months later Britain dropped its insistence on uniformed technicians and an attack on Iran as an additional cause for reactivating the base. Egypt, in turn, agreed to accept an attack on Turkey as an additional cause for reactivating the base and to allow Britain twenty instead of fifteen months in which to complete the withdrawal of its troops. How much both sides lost by the delay need not concern us here. The only important consideration is that both should live up to the spirit as well as the letter of the agreement once it has been signed and ratified.

Just as there are many Egyptians who fear a British betrayal, so, I suppose, there are many Britons who fear an Egyptian betrayal. To such Britons I should like to recall the story that Mahmúd Fawzi, our Minister of Foreign Affairs, told to John Foster Dulles, the American Secretary of State, when he visited Egypt in the spring of 1953 and which I repeated to Adlai Stevenson, the defeated Democratic candidate for President, a few months later. The story, I think, is of Persian origin. It concerns a man named Goha, who deeded his house to another man on condition that he be allowed to examine a certain nail in one of its walls whenever he so desired. The very next day he chose to examine his nail at breakfast time, and of course he was invited to breakfast. The next time he came to examine his nail was lunch time and so he had to be invited to lunch. Soon he began to examine his nail at supper time as well. Then he came to examine it at all hours of the day and night, even when the new owner was not at home and his wife was all alone. Finally, after the man had been carried away to the insane asylum, Goha married his wife, reoccupied the house, and declared himself the owner of all that it contained.

On behalf of the Egyptian people, I would like to say to the British Government: Move out of our house and we'll be your friends, but please don't leave any nails behind or we'll be your enemies forever.

IV

One more problem remains to be settled before Egypt can become a true friend of the West—the problem of Israel, a country whose leaders have systematically and, I fear, successfully misrepresented its position and that of its Arab neighbors. We cannot accept the fact of Israel until its government agrees to revise its frontiers and settle the problem of the Arab refugees in accordance with the various resolutions passed by the United Nations. "Two-thirds of Israel's arable land," an American writer has observed, "is owned by Arab 'absentees'—'absentees' (which means 'refugees'). One-third of the new immigrants to Israel and one-fourth of the total population of Israel live in houses which belong to these 'absentees.' Just about all of Israel's olive groves and half of its citrus groves belong to Arabs now classified as refugees."[9]

[9] I have quoted from an article by John Cogley, the editor of the *Commonweal*, a Catholic weekly published in New York, which appeared in that publication on January 15, 1954. Cogley visited Israel, Egypt, and other countries in the course of a fact-finding tour that was sponsored by the American Friends of the Middle East. He was accompanied by Dr. Harold Fey, the editor of the Protestant *Christian Century*, and by Rabbi Moses Lazarson, the editor of the *Jewish Newsletter*.

It is said that many of the 886,000 refugees in Lebanon, Syria, Jordan, and Egypt can never be resettled inside Israel. But the greater part of them can and must be resettled inside Israel, in preference to new Jewish immigrants, just as the remainder can and must be resettled elsewhere. Israel must fairly compensate those whose property has been seized by others and it must also contribute a fair share to the cost of the resettlement elsewhere of those refugees who are unable or unwilling to be resettled in Israel.

As for Israel's frontiers, we are willing to make adjustments in the interior of the country, where the Jews hold large areas in defiance of the United Nations, in exchange for comparable adjustments on its periphery, provided always that the other Arab states approve of such adjustments and are willing to make similar adjustments of their own. One peripheral adjustment that we must insist upon is the evacuation of southern Negeb, including the supposedly demilitarized "neutral zone" around El Auja, so that Egypt may re-establish its common frontier with Jordan. The Israeli argument that the new port of Elath on the Gulf of Akaba is indispensable, given the Egyptian embargo on Israeli ships and cargoes passing through the Suez Canal, is unsound for three reasons: The Egyptian embargo will be lifted as soon as Israel comes to equitable terms with its Arab neighbors. Shipping in the Gulf of Akaba is controlled by Egyptian batteries along the coast and on various islands, two of which guard the entrance to Elath. Finally, Elath is too far from the economic heart of Israel to justify its existence.

So much for the technical problems, which depend for their solution on the good will of both parties to the argument. Good will on the Arab side, however, depends on the Israelis. We are prepared, as I have said, to make peace with Israel, but only on terms that will not endanger the future of Israel's Arab neighbors or its native inhabitants, the Palestinian Arabs. If there is to be a Jordan Valley Authority, for example, it must serve the interests of Jordan, Syria, and Lebanon in the same proportion as it serves the interests of Israel. If Israel wishes to live in peace with its Arab neighbors, it must call a halt to unrestricted immigration in preparation for military expansion in the future. It must resign itself to a modest role in keeping with its true position in the Middle East. It must renounce, among other things, the imperial ambitions that have inspired so many of its leaders. Israel must convince its Arab neighbors, in short, that it is prepared to live and let live in Middle Eastern terms; that it is not what so many Arabs suspect it of being—the beachhead of a new form of imperialism whose protagonists dream of subjugating, at least economically, the entire Middle East.

If Israel is ever to become self-supporting, it must engage in peaceful trade with the Arab states. Such trade, while not indispensable to the Arab states, would be of benefit to all concerned. The Arab boycott of Israel will continue, however, until such time as we are convinced that the Israelis sincerely wish to dwell in peace among us.

I do not feel that we are being unreasonable in placing the burden of proof on Israel. Israel, after all, is the interloper, the unwelcome neighbor who has appropriated a vital part of our territory by force. Surely we have the right to demand that our new neighbor prove himself a good neighbor before we accept him as a member of our community.

In Egypt, along with our other minorities, are some 85,000 Jews. Those who were born in Egypt or who have opted for Egyptian citizenship enjoy the same rights as other Egyptians. There are no restrictions against Jews in Egypt and there is no

anti-Jewish feeling. The Council of the Revolution has been careful at all times to distinguish between Zionists, who are the partisans of a country with which Egypt is still technically at war,
and the ordinary members of our Jewish community, the great
majority of whom are loyal Egyptian citizens. I think I can safely
say that, in consequence of our policy, relations between Moslems,
Christians, and Jews in Egypt have never been more friendly.
Can Itzhak ben Zvi, the President of Israel, say as much? I ven-
ture to predict that on the day he can it will be easy enough for
Israel to sign a treaty of peace with its Arab neighbors.

V

Assuming that a treaty of peace can be signed with Israel, and
assuming that the Suez Agreement leads to a new era of friendship with Great Britain, the time will come when Egypt, together
with the other members of the League of Arab States, will be
ready to become a full-fledged ally of the West. But we must be
given time and help in order to prepare the conditions for such
an alliance. American spokesmen have often expressed impatience
with the apparent failure of Arab nationalists to appreciate the
magnitude of the Russian threat to the Middle East. I can well
understand their impatience. The fact remains, however, that the
future danger of Russian imperialism, real though it may be, is
less important to us than the present danger of British and French
imperialism. I must therefore say to our American friends: Help
us to free ourselves from the British and the French and we will
do everything we can to co-operate with you in defending ourselves from the Russians.

The United States, as I write, is in the process of negotiating an agreement to provide Egypt with military and economic assistance. Egypt will be expected, in return for such assistance, to cooperate with the United States in preventing Russia from moving into the vacuum left behind by the departing British forces that have hitherto been bottled up in the Suez Canal Zone. So be it. But why allow the vacuum to exist? Why not build up the military strength of the various Arab states to the point necessary to permit their armed forces to defend their own frontiers? A country prepared to defend itself is surely a better ally than a country that must be defended by the armed forces of another country. I realize that it will take a number of years before Egypt and the other Arab countries can be so strengthened as to be able to defend themselves successfully. But unless the effort is made I fear that American plans for defending the Middle East will fail. I repeat: it is only as free peoples capable of defending our freedom that we shall be able and willing to ally ourselves with the West, if the occasion should arise. A regional defense pact on any other terms would merely perpetuate the explosive conditions that now exist. The Americans, instead of gaining allies, would merely inherit the enmity left behind by the British and the French.

I have expressed myself as freely as I have because I believe that the United States is the one power on earth that is capable of dealing with the Arab states on equitable terms. I say this in spite of the partiality that the United States has displayed in the recent past in its dealings with Israel. Now that Great Britain has at last begun to withdraw its forces from the Suez Canal Zone, Israel has begun to oppose the granting of military aid to Egypt or any of the other Arab states on the ground that such aid will endanger its existence. I sincerely hope that the American people will not allow themselves to be taken in by such propaganda. So long as Israel refrains from further aggression, there is little likelihood of its being attacked by Egypt or any of its other Arab neighbors. Egypt, to complete its Revolution, needs the continued support of the West. Why should we jeopardize our good relations with other nations in order to resume the war with Israel—especially at a time when the Arab states are gaining more by means of their economic boycott than they could possibly gain by military means?

Instead of complaining about the non-existent threat of an Arab invasion, the leaders of Israel would do better, I think, to draw up acceptable peace terms to be offered to the members of the League of Arab States. At the moment, the Arab League is devoting most of its energies to enforcing a blockade that is slowly but effectively strangling Israel's economy. Once a satisfactory peace treaty has been signed, however, the blockade will be lifted and Israel will be free to trade with the other members of the Middle Eastern community. The League, for its part, will then be free to devote itself to the purpose for which it was intended—the creation of an Arab federation.

I have continually referred throughout this book to the need for unity, without which neither Egypt nor Sudan nor any other Arab country will be able to overcome the selfish inertia that has been responsible for so many of our common problems. I have referred specifically to the unity of the Nile Valley, on which the prosperity of both Egypt and Sudan depends. The same need for unity has given rise to the concept of a Jordan Valley Authority and, in Syria and Iraq, to the concept of a Tigris-Euphrates Valley Authority. But why stop there? Why should we stop until we have re-created the regional unity that produced the Golden Age of Islam under Harún er Rashíd?

I am enough of an optimist to hope that I shall live to see the day when the League of Arab States becomes a regional federation. The sort of federation that I envision would begin like Bene-lux and end like Switzerland or the United States of America. It would start, as indeed I think it has already started, with a unified foreign policy, and proceed from there to a customs union that would in turn produce a unified economy and, eventually, a single passport and a single military establishment. Each Arab state would respect the political autonomy of the others. The federation would be governed by a parliamentary regime that would change its capital and its cabinet every year or two by turn. Only thus, I think, will it be possible for the Arab peoples to mobilize the power necessary to make their voices clearly heard in the councils of the world.

VI

But I must return to Egypt, whose destiny is the subject of this book. In so doing, however, I would like to express the convic-tion that the destiny of Egypt will largely determine the destiny of the entire Middle East. All of the problems of the Middle East ex-ist in Egypt in concentrated form. To the extent that the Council of the Revolution succeeds in solving Egypt's problems, it will set an example for the other Arab states to follow. To the extent that it fails to solve Egypt's problems, it will delay the solution of the same sort of problems in the other Arab states for a long time to come. In conclusion, therefore, I shall attempt to summarize the more important achievements of the Egyptian Revolution.

We inherited from the old regime a deficit in the balance of international payments that amounted in 1952 to LE 55,400,000 ($158,998,000). Thanks to our austerity program, which in-cluded severe restrictions on foreign travel and imported con-

sumer goods, we were able to reduce the deficit in 1953 to LE 8,-
300,000 ($23,821,000). By the end of the first half of 1954,
after converting the deficit into a small surplus, we relaxed the
austerity program to the extent of permitting limited foreign travel
and the importation of limited quantities of the more essential
consumer goods.

Our budget for the year 1954–55, the largest in the history of
Egypt, has been balanced, thanks to continued austerity and
increased taxation, at approximately LE 288,000,000 ($824,560,-
000). Of this amount, approximately LE 60,000,000 ($173,922,-
000) consists of extraordinary expenditures designed to expedite
the Revolution. Approximately one fourth of this amount is being
spent on projects designed to improve the health of the Egyptian
people; the remaining three quarters is being spent on projects
designed to increase production.

The largest health expenditures include LE 5,400,000 for the
installation of potable wells in the villages; LE 4,500,000 for the
construction of rural "multiple-service units," which consist of
primary schools combined with clinics, libraries, and recreation
centers; LE 1,150,000 for tuberculosis hospitals; and LE 1,000,-
000 for clinics and recreation centers in the industrial areas that
most require them.

The largest expenditures designed to increase production include LE 17,700,000 for reclaiming and improving agricultural
lands; LE 10,800,000 for improving communications; LE 4,150,-
000 for increasing cereal and animal production; and LE 2,700,-
000 for increasing the production of petroleum and other min-
erals.

In addition to these extraordinary expenditures, LE 4,825,000
is being spent on the construction of primary and secondary
schools; LE 4,225,000 is being spent on the administration of

the agrarian reforms; and LE 3,525,000 is being spent on improving the facilities of the universities of Cairo and Alexandria and the institutions for religious education associated with the University of El Azhar.

A part of the sums I have mentioned is being spent in connection with projects supervised by the United States Technical Cooperation Administration. In three years the United States Government has contributed $14,481,273 to Point Four projects in Egypt. The more important of these projects, to which the Egyptian Government has contributed $21,362,942 in the same period of time, include the growing of seeds for the production of hybrid corn; the importation of baby chicks to improve and increase egg and poultry production; a survey of Egypt's water resources; and a survey of its industrial potential.

Two executive agencies have been created to supervise the rapid development of Egypt's economy. The first, the National Resources Development Board, has been placed in charge of all basic projects. The second, the National Production Council, has been placed in charge of all projects capable of being completed during the ten-year plan. During the first half of the ten-year plan, approximately LE 200,000,000 ($574,000,000) will be spent at the rate of LE 40,000,000 a year on such projects as the following:

In addition to power stations in North Cairo, Talkha, and Idfu, which were begun under the old regime, and which will be completed before the end of 1955, the low dam at Asswan is at long last being converted to the production of electricity and artificial fertilizer. Two more power stations are being erected in South Cairo. The electrification of the low dam could and should have been completed years ago. It was only the corrupt politics of the old regime that prevented its initiation until after the Revolution. Together the six projects will cost about LE 40,-000,000 ($114,800,000). The Asswan project, which alone will cost LE 27,500,000 ($78,950,000), will be completed early in 1958. It will consist of seven turbines, each capable of producing 46,000 kilowatts per hour, or an estimated annual total (allowing for seasonal variations in the level of the Nile) of approximately 1,900,000,000 kilowatt-hours, plus a factory capable of an annual production of 370,000 tons of artificial fertilizer.

Inasmuch as the fertilizer factory will consume about 1,350,-000,000 kilowatt-hours of current per year, only 550,000,000 kilowatt-hours will be available for domestic and industrial use in other parts of Egypt. Hence our desire to begin as soon as possible the construction of the new high dam at Kalabsha, the plans for which have already been completed with the help of the Technical Cooperation Administration. The high dam, in addition to producing the water necessary to increase Egypt's tillable acreage by from 30 to 60 per cent, will also produce an additional 10,000,000,000 kilowatt-hours of electricity per year—enough to cover Egypt's industrial and domestic needs for a generation. The high dam, as I have said, will cost LE 180,000,000 ($516,-600,000). If we could obtain a loan of $250,000,000 from the International Bank for Reconstruction and Development, to cover the cost of the machinery and other equipment that would have to be imported, we could handle the remainder of the cost ourselves.

The new fertilizer plant at Asswan is expected to save LE 4,000,000 per year—the difference in cost between 370,000 tons of imported and domestic fertilizer. Such savings could be used in helping to defray the cost of building the high dam. And, if and when the high dam is built, the fertilizer plant could be expanded to the extent necessary to supply all domestic needs over and above those already being supplied by the Egyptian Fertilizer and Industrial Chemical Company's factory at Suez. The erection of the Suez plant, which produces 200,000 tons of fertilizer every year from the waste gases of the local oil refineries, was financed with the help of a loan from the Export-Import Bank of the United States. The same company, which is controlled by Ahmed Abbúd, will also operate the Asswan fertilizer factory for the government.

On February 11, 1954, a company called the Egyptian Iron and Steel Works, Incorporated, was formed for the purpose of erecting and operating at Helwan, sixteen miles south of Cairo, a plant capable of an annual production of 220,000 tons of billets, girders, ties, plates, sheets, and rails. The company was formed in spite of the advice of certain foreign experts, who argued that steel cannot be economically produced in Egypt. Only time will tell. The government, for its part, is so confident that steel can be economically produced in Egypt that it has contributed LE 2,000,000 of the LE 15,000,000 that will eventually be invested in the enterprise. To encourage the sale of shares to private investors, moreover, the government has guaranteed a minimum dividend of 4 per cent as from the third year after the company's incorporation. The government has also agreed to guarantee the repayment of the nominal value of all bonds sold up to LE 4,000,-000. German firms have been engaged to erect and equip the plant.

The iron ore, which will be mined near Asswan, will be brought down the Nile in barges to be smelted at Helwan. Although imported coke will cost twice what it costs in Europe, the ore delivered at Helwan will cost less than half of what it costs in Europe. Eventually, we hope, it will be possible to smelt iron economically with the electricity produced by the high dam.

Pig iron instead of ore could then be shipped by barge to the plant at Helwan.

I have been an enthusiastic supporter of an Egyptian iron and steel industry ever since 1945, when I was the governor of the Eastern Desert. The ore from the Asswan deposits, whose proved reserves total 168,000,000 tons, averages 48 per cent pure iron; it is thus much richer than most of the ores now being used in Europe. Another large deposit of iron, of which I also made a personal study, is located near Wadi Kereim, about twenty miles southwest of Kosseir on the Red Sea. The magnetite ore at Wadi Kereim averages 45 per cent pure iron. It also averages 25 per cent silica, which means that it cannot be smelted until most of the silica has been removed.

In spite of such difficulties, however, I am hopeful that Egypt can produce iron and steel economically. With all the experiments that are now going on, in Scandinavia and elsewhere in western Europe, it cannot be long before an economical process of smelting iron in electric furnaces is discovered. When that day comes our basic problem will be solved. In the meantime, even if we have to produce expensive iron and steel with imported coke, we will have laid the foundations of a semi-industrial economy.

India, Turkey, and South Africa have all been partially industrialized in the present century. Why shouldn't Egypt also be industrialized to some extent? Egypt lacks abundant fuel and mineral resources and must therefore remain a predominantly agricultural country. But there is no reason why it shouldn't benefit from the exploitation of the mineral resources that it does possess. Agriculture alone can never produce a decent standard of living. Industry offers the only hope of improving the conditions of life in Egypt, a country that has been described in the past as "an economic vacuum in an industrial desert."

The vacuum is now being filled. With the help of Point Four, we are prospecting for copper, lead, zinc, tin, and antimony, as well as for chromium, molybdenum, tungsten, and nickel. We are already producing manganese, mostly for the United States, and we are preparing to produce titanium from a large and rich deposit of ilmenite near Wadi Ranga. But, most of all, in the absence of any known coal reserves, we are encouraging the search for oil.

Unlike some of its Arab neighbors, Egypt is not a large producer of petroleum. In recent years, in fact, our production has been decreasing, largely in consequence of the restrictive legislation of the old regime. In the hope of increasing production to the point of self-sufficiency and, if possible, to beyond that point, we have liberalized the so-called mining law and signed a series of exploration agreements with various American and British oil companies. We are also increasing the capacity of the government-owned refinery at Suez from 300,000 to 1,300,000 tons per year, and we have engaged an Italian firm to build a pipeline from Suez to Cairo in order to reduce the cost of the fuel oil consumed by our industrial establishments.

In order to encourage the investment of both foreign and domestic capital in Egypt, we have amended the provision of the so-called company law, also enacted during the monarchy, which required 51 per cent of the shares in all companies to be held by Egyptians. The amended law merely requires that 49 per cent of the shares be reserved for Egyptian investors for one month after a company's incorporation. At the end of that time any shares still available may be held by anyone. The shares in any new company whose activities are likely to increase national production without competing with any existing company may be wholly owned by foreigners. Whereas the old law forbade the repatriation of capital before the end of twenty years, at a rate not exceeding 10 per cent in any one year after the tenth year from the date of incorporation, the new law permits the repatriation of capital in eight years at a rate not exceeding 20 per cent in any one year after the third year from the date of incorporation. Profits may now be repatriated, after the payment of taxes, in the currency of the foreigner contributing the capital. And, finally, all new companies financed with foreign capital have been exempted from taxation during the first five years following their incorporation.

As the result of such favorable legislation, several new foreign companies have been formed in Egypt since the Revolution for the discovery and eventual production of petroleum. Other new companies, some foreign and some Egyptian, have been formed for the manufacture of rubber tires, automobile batteries, pharmaceuticals, and textiles, and a new company for the manufacture of paper from bagasse (a crushed sugar cane) is now in the process of formation.

While relaxing the restrictions on capital, both foreign and domestic, we have also decreed new laws for the protection of labor. Both agricultural and industrial unions are being encouraged so long as they refrain from political agitation. Labor disputes in vital industries are subject to compulsory arbitration; a cooling-off period of fifteen days has been prescribed in other industries; and no strike is permissible in any industry unless conciliation has failed. At the same time, industrial workers are now protected against arbitrary dismissals. They are also guaranteed an annual two-week vacation with pay as well as sick-leave benefits, social insurance, and pensions. Labor exchanges have been established in Cairo, Alexandria, and other cities for the purpose of combating unemployment. Public housing projects, complete with clinics, schools, and recreation areas, are being

financed out of the proceeds—LE 75,000,000 ($215,200,000)—
resulting from the confiscation of the property of King Faruk
and other members of the royal family. New urban schools are
being erected at the rate of 300 a year and new dormitories are
being built for students in the technical schools and universities.

The political situation still leaves much to be desired, but I
am confident that by the end of the transitional period, in January
1956, the Council of the Revolution will have begun to restore
the liberties of which the people have been deprived. Drastic
problems require drastic solutions. Although Egypt is being governed by a military dictatorship, the dictatorship has resisted the
temptation to nationalize the economy. On the contrary, it has
done everything possible to encourage private initiative, both foreign and domestic. Although I have differed with my junior colleagues on many occasions, I shall continue to support them so
long as they continue to work for the goals of the Egyptian Revolution, among the most important of which are to raise the standard of living by increasing production and to make it possible for
the people to participate in Egypt's social, political, and economic
development without distinction as to class, race, sex, or creed.

What has been done in Egypt can be done in the other Arab
countries, and especially in those with large revenues from oil
production, with the proper encouragement from abroad. Egypt
is the most populous and most productive of the Arab countries,
and, because it is, its problems are at once more difficult and
easier to solve than those of the more backward countries. But
the basic problems are everywhere the same—poverty, illiteracy,
and disease, and the emotional frustrations resulting from too
many years of irresponsible government and oppressive foreign
intervention. If the West wishes to assist in the creation of a
healthy and friendly Middle East, the time has come to ponder

the lessons of the Egyptian Revolution and apply them elsewhere. The other countries may not blindly follow Egypt's example, but, except for the issue of monarchy versus republic, which will have to be settled in accordance with local realities, I am reasonably certain that their behavior will be roughly the same. The West, I think, will do well to help them rather than hinder them in their struggle to achieve their destinies as Egypt is struggling to achieve its own. The revolt of the Arab peoples, after all, is but a belated reflection of the revolt of the Western peoples that began with the revolutions in the United States and France.

INDEX